For the past 35 years Chr[...]
failing) to make a livin[...]
playwright and, most rece[...]
nine novels, one work of [...]
numerous short stories al[...]
full-time as a radio producer at the BBC.

After serious reflection and some research, Paling has discovered he is the UK and Commonwealth's 1001st Most Important Novelist (Living). However, he acknowledges that it's unlikely you will have any idea who he is.

Praise for *A Very Nice Rejection Letter*

'Like all good diarists Paling's musings are funny, tender and uncensored'

Sunday Times

'Funny and revealing . . . everyone who is convinced they have a book in them should read [this book]'

Mail on Sunday

'A Very Nice Rejection Letter is a completely authentic account of what it's like to be merely reasonably good'

Literary Review

'Splendidly entertaining'

The Chap

A Very Nice Rejection Letter

Diary of a Novelist

Chris Paling

CONSTABLE

CONSTABLE

First published in Great Britain in 2021 by Constable
This paperback edition published in 2022 by Constable

13 5 7 9 10 8 6 4 2

A CIP catalogue record for this book
is available from the British Library.

ISBN: 978-1-47213-488-2

Typeset in Calluna by SX Composing DTP, Rayleigh, Essex
Printed and bound in Great Britain by Clays Ltd, Elcograf, S.p.A.

Papers used by Constable are from well-managed forests
and other responsible sources.

Constable
An imprint of
Little, Brown Book Group
Carmelite House
50 Victoria Embankment
London EC4Y 0DZ

An Hachette UK Company

www.hachette.co.uk

www.littlebrown.co.uk

For Anita

'You're just hiding from reality,' Becker said.

'Why not?'

'You'll never be a writer if you hide from reality.'

'What are you talking about? That's what writers *do*.'

Ham on Rye Charles Bukowski

... One day I started writing, not knowing that I had chained myself for life to a noble but merciless master. When God hands you a gift, he also hands you a whip; and the whip is intended solely for self-flagellation.

Music for Chameleons Truman Capote

Contents

Contents

Part 1

Diary 2007 & 2008

There are three rules for the writing of a novel. Unfortunately, nobody knows what they are.

W. Somerset Maugham

2007

6th April

Writing income this year so far (my tax year runs from the end of January) is, give or take a pound or two, minus £300. The deficit is due to the fact that I paid my accountant £348 for preparing last year's risible accounts and so far have earned only £49.52 from the ALCS – an august body which chases up bits of copyright here and there on the writer's behalf. I am, however, owed £1000 from Portobello Books (less agent's commission and VAT), which represents the final part of the dismal advance for my upcoming novel, *Minding*.

Despite the unpromising financial situation, after twenty-odd years trying to make a living on and around Grub Street – several novels published to grudgingly respectful reviews ('Among the most accomplished novelists to emerge in recent years' the *Independent* – a quote that's been hauled out and dusted off on numerous occasions I might add) and negligible sales – I feel that this might just be the year in which something happens. Then again it might not. But hope drives all writers on.

A recent survey revealed the average British novelist's yearly income to be something around £8000 – but weep no tears for the professional novelist. It's a profession perpetually in crisis, overburdened by vanity and under-served by talent. The age of ludicrous advances is over, longstanding writers are being canned by their publishers and the public's taste has become impossible to second-guess. Getting a publisher today is more dependent than ever on getting an agent, and agents are more choosy than they have ever been. They therefore hold more power than they have ever done and a growing number are chancing their hands at writing, while many publishers are jumping ship and becoming agents or writers. *Publishing rule 1: Be wary of a published agent. Whatever they profess, their attention will never be far from their own work.*

Novel writing aside, writing for the screen is of course the Holy Grail to the impoverished novelist. Having had a great deal of contact with the film and TV industries over the past few years I can report that they are generally staffed by hugely enthusiastic (everything is *awesome*, *beautiful* or *sublime*), wildly self-confident but generally powerless people. It's an 'on spec' industry, which means the writer may well put in many years' work for absolutely no financial reward. But of course if you do strike gold then it's all worth it which is why otherwise relatively sane people are happy to prostitute themselves shamelessly.

Six months ago I was clearing out a cupboard and came across sixty pages of one of my old film scripts, *Ivan and the Dead Guy,* a noir road movie about a medical student, a terminal young boy and a corpse. I can't remember why it was abandoned, but I sat down to read it, fully expecting to consign it to the recycling bin, only to find it wasn't at all bad. So I wrote another thirty pages and sent it off to

4

my film agent, Fay. She thought it worked too and punted it to various companies. She said it was a good 'calling card' script. *Publishing rule 2: A calling card script is one deemed good enough to earn you a meeting with a film company in Soho.* Film meetings are the equivalent of the dinners those entering the legal profession are obliged to take at the Inns of Court. (Until you've had a number of them you won't be granted access to the profession.)

Last week I was granted a meeting with one of the powerful BBC TV commissioners to discuss *Ivan*. This came as something of a surprise because he'd had the script for six months and although it had earned an appreciative email from a producer there the commissioner she had in mind for it never seemed to get around to reading it. Out of frustration I emailed the producer direct and she emailed back to say that this had prompted her to remind the man in charge about the script. He got back to her (he was, of course, in the States making deals) and told her to set up a meeting. After four cancellations, which I took to be a bad sign, I finally met Kenton and the producer. Kenton immediately asked if he could be brutal. I assured him that he could, in response to which he said, 'There's no way on earth this would ever get made as a film, the idea isn't big enough.' At this point I stood, thanking him for his time and readying myself to leave. He then said, 'But . . .'

The 'but' led to a conversation in which he and the producer discussed the possibility of cutting it by thirty pages (the thirty pages I'd recently added perhaps) and running it in the planned new *Comedy Playhouse* series. 'How would you feel about that?' I told him I'd feel OK about that, and I presumed I'd be working 'on spec' as usual – i.e., lots of work for no return. But, he said, 'No, I think it would be unfair to ask you to do that.'

'Good,' I said.

So they're going to option the script for a small fee, pay something for the rewrite and then pay a bit more if it gets made. The other plus side to this is that the series is also a trawl for potentially longer-running series – so essentially these are six pilots. Kenton asked, therefore, if I'd mind not killing off my two main characters at the end. I said I wouldn't mind that at all (although in truth I'd forgotten that I had, not having read the script for a few months).

It's now Easter so everybody has gone away and this being Grub Street means long holidays. Grub Street's year is exceptionally short. Agents and publishers are habitually either gearing up or recovering from the Frankfurt or London book fairs. Three days in Frankfurt tends to wipe them out for at least a month . . . who knows what goes on there.

25th April

I've already been a bit lax keeping this journal. In fact it was only this morning that I remembered I'd decided to keep a record of the year. It's the hottest spring on record apparently so most people are operating at reduced capacity. So far I have spotted three wasps in the kitchen. Not sure where they came from but they seemed very tired and not very yellow. I put them in the garden where I imagine they have found somewhere to sleep for another month or so. It reminds me of a question from my son when he was small, possibly the title of his autobiography should he ever get around to writing it (he's only fifteen so it's a bit early to tell). The question he asked was, 'Are bees made of meat?' When he was small – maybe four – he gave me the title for my third novel. It was a winter's afternoon and, apropos of nothing, he said, 'It's been morning all day, today,' then he went on playing. I knew what he meant and immediately borrowed *Morning all Day* and it remains my favourite title.

In terms of the screenplays currently doing the rounds, things are not looking too promising for *When the Whales Came In*. This is a full-length script set in South Australia and is 'in development' (but not yet optioned) with a respectable UK company and attached to a promising young director (PYD) looking to follow up his first two films. The development executive for the company was due back from maternity leave mid-April, at which point she'd promised to chivvy everybody along and get the project moving again. I hadn't heard anything by the twenty-first so emailed her. By return I got an ominous email from her PA asking me for a telephone number the producer could reach me on the following day. She duly called to tell me that a week before she was due to return from maternity leave she left the company. However, she assured me that she was keen to work on it as an independent producer, feels that unfettered by company bureaucracy she'll be able to give it more time and effort, and if I was happy she'd call the promising young British director and set up a meeting. Two days elapsed and I hadn't heard anything so I emailed PYD again – an appeal to his sense of decency (I have, after all, written seven drafts of the thing without complaint and listened to all of his suggestions and, indeed, incorporated them all) – but have, as of today, had no reply.

Another film script, *Thought About You*, recently sent out by Fay to another young British director, has met with approval. The director got back to her quickly, declaring it 'stupendous' and asking for two weeks to give it some thought. However, the two weeks have now elapsed and the presumption has to be that he's found something more stupendous to work on. Fay bumped into an American producer at the London Book Fair and punted him the idea. He liked it enough to ask her to email the script to him. He's back in New York this week so we'll see if he's interested. Chances, of course, are nil.

As requested by the BBC I've now cut *Ivan and the Dead Guy* to sixty pages but Fay is still arguing over the option fee, the rewrite fee and whether these will be set against final payment. If it gets made I'll get about £10,000. If it doesn't I'll get around £1000 (minus commission, minus VAT). Anything would be welcome as my ledgers are still showing a minus figure for the current financial year.

27th April

Minding, the new novel, is out in just over two weeks' time which provokes the usual feelings of anxiety and depression in me. A few books back I diagnosed why this occurred: it's the way I protect myself from the inevitable disappointment following publication. This does tend to sap the joy from the arrival of a new book and I wish there was something I could do to prevent it, but at the moment there isn't.

I have so far published seven novels with the hardback house Jonathan Cape and the paperback imprint, Vintage, who continued to support me until my editor finally admitted defeat to the marketing department and let me go – i.e., sacked me. It becomes harder for an editor to enlist the support of marketing for a new book when an author's figures are flat-lining. *Publishing rule 3: Lack of support from the marketing department is often used as the excuse when editors fire authors.*

The relationship between a writer and a publisher hovers somewhere between that of dog and owner – each party taking a turn to hold the lead. When I last spotted my ex-publisher he was lunching with an American bigwig whose face I recognised. It felt like a huge betrayal. *Publishing rule 4: Publishers and agents always pay for lunch which means that writers, though generally impoverished, enjoy occasional glimpses into some of the swankiest restaurants in London. Publishing rule 5: The publisher or agent always chooses the restaurant. The writer can therefore work out how highly he's regarded by the size of the lunch bill and the length of the lunch. This is of benefit not only to the writer but also the publisher who can enjoy a lunch he wouldn't usually be able to afford.*

I suspect Jonathan Cape held on to me for several novels longer than was economically wise for them. This is the typical career trajectory of what is deemed a mid-list novelist. *Publishing rule 6: There is no such thing as a low-list novelist.* A mid-lister is someone who showed early promise but failed to hit the sales or prize jackpot.

I was therefore lucky to be taken on by Portobello Books in the shape of Tasja who saw the manuscript of *Minding* and liked it enough to take a chance on it.

Publishing is one of the few industries that routinely releases new products onto the market without an advertising budget. Companies live in the hope that reviews will sell the books – and trigger the mythical 'word of mouth' that occasionally catapults obscure tracts onto the bestseller lists. *Captain Corelli*, *Curious Incident* and *The Island* are usually trotted out as examples of this (though all of these actually had a decent marketing spend) – while the other thirty-odd-thousand books released during the same period for which this didn't swing into action doesn't seem to dent their belief in it. This, of course, is a personal view but one that I know is shared by many other writers. Publishers I think would argue that books will find their own readership and if a readership is not there then they can't manufacture one out of thin air. However, the more they've spent on a book the harder they try.

A number of factors must come into play for a book to find a readership and sell in reasonable numbers. Advertising can help but reviews and word of mouth are critical. The book has to hit the zeitgeist and to do this it needs a tight clutch of positive reviews, appearances on radio and/or TV either plugging the book directly or obliquely as a pundit, newspaper extracts, supporting pieces in the press written by the author (top five books, favourite restaurant, anything in the book's narrative that can be tied to the current news agenda), news pieces (rare but very useful), bookshop appearances, web visibility (costly but definitely worthwhile), social media excitement, bookshop promotion, author stunts (accident, early death, arrest etc.), Radio 4 adaptation, support of fellow writers or public figures (proofs are mailed out ahead of publication to anybody in the world who has at some point said something positive about a previous book or the author) and anything else the overworked publicist can come up with.

Tasja has so far failed to answer any of my emails asking if she's managed to blag the book into WHSmith or into the supermarkets. I do know, however, it has gone off in a bundle to be considered for the 'Richard & Judy Bookclub' on TV. An appearance on that list guarantees promotion and significant sales. On top of those benefits the writer is lucky enough to get his or her book dissected on the sofa by the fine minds of Richard and Judy and a couple of C-list celebs. It's deeply unsettling seeing the set-up film of the non-televisual, badly dressed author, stumbling around a muddy urban wood and trying to make his/her book sound more interesting than it actually is. Madeley (semi-tanned in tightly cut suit, nice white shirt, no tie) then usually picks up the book from the coffee table, taps it with his lengthy forefinger, and gets the review under-way with his assessment of its literary merit. Judy's is often the shrewder and more considered view, but she doesn't get too long to talk before Madeley is back with his second opinion. He then talks over the celebs, plonks the book back on the coffee table, taps it again and delivers the killer final verdict.

Minding has, however, been getting some good pre-publication responses and a producer from a Liverpool TV company has read it, is coming to London next week, and is keen to meet to discuss the possibility of them doing something with it. That's next Wednesday.

29th April

Word back from film agent Fay from the young British film director ('stupendous'). He has considered *Thought About You* and has decided not to take it on. While he still likes the writing and characterisation he can't make the

100 per cent connection with it that will warrant him spending the next two or three years trying to get the money to make it. Fair enough, at least he got back to us with an honest appraisal (unlike the other PYD). He wishes me luck and to be 'kept in the loop' of what I am doing.

The *Independent* has asked me to do a 'Book of a Lifetime' column to tie in with publication of *Minding*. The *Indy* is the only national newspaper to have carried reviews of all of my books and even sent Nick Royle to interview me for the last one. Good writer – undeservedly obscure. I also had my photograph taken in Cavendish Square, just behind Oxford Street. Inadvisedly I was wearing a light-coloured mac so looked like a sinister park lurker. For some reason the photographer asked me to raise both my arms a bit so it looks as if I'm about to try and launch myself into the air. It reminded me of the author photo shoot for my first novel. I protested that I didn't want my ugly mug on the inside back cover but they insisted and sent me to a smart house in North London where a woman photographed me for two hours and tried to make me look moody and interesting. She failed, but the photo with me smoking a cigarette was deemed acceptable. The photo was taken around 1994 so at least I look relatively young. Trade paperbacks don't tend to use one. *Publishing rule 7: The trade paperback has been a boon to unphotogenic authors.*

The *Indy*'s interest in my *oeuvre* is in contrast to the *Observer* that, for some perverse reason, has managed only two reviews (one of which was fewer than ten words – 'Paling is a name to watch') over the past fifteen years. I've already done *Pierre et Jean* by Guy de Maupassant for the *Guardian* some years ago (everybody always chooses

Flaubert's *Madame Bovary*) so I've decided to do the short stories of Raymond Carver. He manages to achieve more in ten pages than most novelists do in three hundred.

The commission prompted me to go back to some of his collections and reread them. In *Cathedral* I found a story I didn't remember, 'The Compartment'. The protagonist is a man going to Strasbourg to visit the son he hasn't seen for years, the son whose malign interference, he reckons, hastened the end of his marriage; an interesting glimpse into Carver's psychology. There was no love lost between father and son but he's recently had a letter out of the blue signed off with a casual 'Love . . .' so he decides to take a few weeks' leave from his job, visit Europe and catch up with him. They arrange to meet at a railway station. On the train journey the expensive watch he has bought for his son is stolen from the train compartment. When he reaches the station he knows he can't face the boy so he stays on the train and leaves without renewing the acquaintance. Something in it that really struck me, given the British obsession and unwavering love for Venice, was the dismissal of the city after spending a day there: 'Venice was a disappointment. He saw a man with one arm eating fried squid, and there were grimy water-stained buildings everywhere he looked.' Writers should always particularise – choose the telling detail to bring things to life. The one-armed man in Venice seems to do it as well as anything.

I've just finished redrafting the *Whales* film script as a novel which raised a number of issues about character and setting. This was an interesting process. Kingsley Amis likened novel writing to taking a journey from London to Edinburgh without a map (I think it was

Edinburgh, I think it was Kingsley Amis). He knew the first fifty miles by heart and he knew the destination. The interesting bit was the three-hundred-odd other miles you had to travel discovering the route for yourself. With *Whales* (or *North of Anxious Bay* as the novel is called), the story was there before I began so the fleshing out process of character and setting was the more interesting part of the process. Deborah, my literary agent, has now had draft two for five weeks and I await her verdict on whether we should punt it out to some publishers to test the water.

3rd May

Meeting yesterday with the development producer from the Liverpool TV company keen on *Minding*. They have a couple of regular network programmes which bring in an income stream and want to develop some single dramas. The producer has worked on various soaps and is convinced she can get something going with the book. The head of the company has now got it and she's awaiting his verdict.

The format of such meetings is this: you walk enthusiastically into the chilly Soho office of a young, usually female, producer, usually with a head cold, whose desk is neatly stacked with scripts and adorned with framed photographs of her nieces and nephews. She will be wearing skinny jeans, torn artfully at the knees, a long expensive cashmere cardigan, a diaphanous scarf (usually reddish in colour) and drinking fruit tea or Lemsip from a large mug, around which, for the duration of the meeting, her chilly white fingers will be wrapped. There will be a large leather handbag, slightly open, on the floor at the top of which her mobile phone will be perched, screen angled up so she can monitor her phone traffic by glancing down and therefore not appearing rude. There will be a large bottle of mineral water partially hidden by the scripts on the desk and a box of tissues perched on top of them. Propped against the slightly grubby walls will be framed posters of big British films you've heard of but, because they are British films, are unlikely to have bothered to go out to see. Rarely will these posters be hung on the walls. The film industry is precarious; premises are routinely abandoned every three or four months. So, once you sit down and decline the half-hearted offer of coffee, the producer sneezes then runs through what her company has on its 'slate'. These are projects with optioned scripts in various stages of completion awaiting finance. Those that are nearly ready to go will have a director attached and will be awaiting a big actor to sign up before finance is forthcoming (this being a British film – and 2007 – chances are that actor will be Clive Owen – TV's *Chancer* – who, for some absurd reason, despite having only one expression – rugged incredulity – has become bankable in movie terms). After the slate has been run through by the producer or development person it's your turn. You talk a bit about your script and other projects, she then explains to you that your script is not quite right for them, but thanks you for coming in, gives you her card, tells you to keep in touch (i.e., don't). Then you go away. If you ever do try to reach her in the future chances are she will be 'at home, reading' or have moved to another company.

Also heard from *Whales*' potential producer S. to say that she's finally made contact with PYD who apologises for not being in touch but he is keen to meet on his return from Spain and LA. He's happy for her to take the *Whales* project on as an independent and so things can start moving on again. I'm meeting S. tomorrow to catch up face to face.

Meanwhile, *Minding* is out in eight days. Feel the usual mix of despair and elation. All writers are flawed – otherwise they'd get on with the business of living rather than watching other people live and writing about them. Those who feel the urge to write (fiction in particular) have a peculiar need to be heard in a certain way. If, therefore, you write and your books don't sell or reach an audience, then they're not doing the job. Seems a fatuous reason but I think this is the core of it – screaming in the dark for your mother to lift you out of the cot.

Early review of *Minding* in the *New Humanist*. A good mag driven along by Laurie Taylor who attracts some seriously good contributors with the reward of a few quid or six bottles of decent wine per piece. He employed me as a book reviewer for a year or so. The review is very positive bar one or two niggles. *Publishing rule 8: It's the niggles you remember.* The *Mail* is expected on Friday and some others are in the offing – *The Times* and the *Guardian*, maybe. The *Express* is running a thousand-word story I wrote and are doing a reader's offer. I enjoyed writing the story – a thousand words is a good discipline.

Oh yes. £400 has just arrived from the *Guardian* for a book review so for the first time this year the writing ledger is in the black to the tune of £20 or so.

31st October

As predicted *Minding* came and went to a small flurry of generally positive reviews. I think it sold about three thousand copies. Not bad in the current climate, but not exactly in the *Da Vinci Code* bracket. Tasja worked hard at getting it out there. It made a couple of summer promotions but has now disappeared from the shops and languishes at number 165,000 in the Amazon sales rankings. *Publishing rule 9: To authors, the Amazon sales ranking is the equivalent of the Saturday football results ticker on TV. Authors watch it like a hawk. Every sale influences your position. A single sale can catapult you a hundred thousand places. Obviously the higher you get the more copies you have to sell to progress – but it's a great displacement activity.* My highest point was 105 for *Newton's Swing* ('My hope for the Booker. . .' the *Indy*).

The films are all currently dormant. No further emails on *Whales*. PYD and the canned producer have both gone to ground – and neither is returning emails. *Publishing rule 10: In the film industry, as in life I suppose, if you have to ask the question the answer is usually no.*

A brief flurry of interest in *Ivan*, though it failed at the commissioning meeting at the BBC so that's the end of that. The BBC works in a way that could be seen as perverse and wasteful from the outside. Internal departments put time and money into projects which they then try to sell to other people within the BBC – the powerful commissioners. If projects are turned down, as they often are, the time and money are wasted. The commissioners liked the writing apparently and would like to see more. There is no more except for this journal and I don't think they'd find much of interest in here (this is deemed a 'hostage to fortune' line to literary critics). Fay called the BBC for feedback but no response. I have, however, written a new screenplay based on *Newton's Swing* ('My hope for the Booker . . .'). It's called *An American Cockroach*. I think it works. Fay thinks it works. She sent it out a couple of months ago and we're waiting for the companies to start tearing each other apart in a bidding frenzy. I'm sure it'll happen – given time. There has, apparently, been a call from a smart British company who only distribute films but who are rumoured to be looking to produce. The man liked the script a lot but is busy for a few weeks and promises to get back to us when he isn't.

The Booker has come and gone again. *Minding* of course failed to trouble the longlist. I thus remain the only living British novelist never to be shortlisted (or indeed long-listed) for any literary prize, receive any bursary or grant, attend any Arvon course, have any foreign publisher or appear at any literary festival. I watched thirty seconds of the ceremony on the TV news in bed and saw Anne Enright collect the cheque. All they managed to cover of her speech was 'Well . . .' before cutting back to Fiona in the studio (who nowadays seems to have taken to delivering the evening news standing up, giving hand signals like a deaf interpreter – perhaps she gets an enhanced fee for it). Says it all really. 'Well . . .' My wife, Julie, was in the en suite and asked why I was shouting at the television. Then she came in and saw it was the Booker result and said, 'Oh.'

Email silence from both agent and publisher. Five emails unresponded to from Deborah, three from Tasja at Portobello. What agents and publishers have never understood (or perhaps they understand only too well), is that writers need contact not when their books are being published but when they're not. Midlist writers fall off the radar when they have nothing in the review columns.

They cease to exist. Popular writers, by contrast, are always around in 'What I did on my holidays' columns (free holidays paid for by PR companies in return for a few photos and a thousand words of dashed-off copy explaining how brilliant was the hotel/location/flight), 'Best of the Year' lists, *Call My Bluff* or *A Good Read*.

My day job is Radio 4 producer. Over a long career I've worked on many daily and weekly programmes as well as talks and documentaries. I'm currently producing *Midweek,* the weekly live chat show presented by Libby Purves. She tells me of her agent, the legendary Hilary Rubinstein, who was often on the phone. She and her husband, then running a farm, categorised this as 'lambing'. This is what a farmer does during the lambing season, walking round the sheds several times a night, lifting tails, checking for the bloody head of a new life to begin to emerge.

On a positive note I have been asked to appear at the Bath Literature Festival next year with a writer called Patrick Gale. We're both apparently 'leading British novelists at the peak of our powers'. The programme copy was sent for approval and I enthusiastically approved it. Having never spoken at a literary festival, let alone visited one, I have no idea what I'll say. I'm hopeless at talking off the cuff so will probably write something that sounds off the cuff, perhaps on my cuff. Must buy a white shirt for the occasion. It's all quite terrifying but it might shift a couple of copies of *Minding* and Julie says it will be good for me to do.

Incidentally I went to see Peter Messer last weekend. Peter is a very good painter who works in egg tempera (an ancient technique in which pigment is mixed with egg yolk as a carrier medium). He was talking at the 'Lewes Live' literary festival. We have a few of Peter's paintings we bought when we used to have money to spend and I wanted to see him because of something I'm working on at the moment. For an hour he sat on the stage in an old Lewes hotel, rain pouring down outside, in front of a huge screen onto which his work was projected. He talked quietly and compellingly about what it is to be an artist and earned huge applause. He works, lives and drinks in an area of less than a square mile. His recent work has all featured this square mile: the bowling green at dawn, the walls of the animal pens behind Lewes Castle. A path and a streetlight. A line that stuck with me was something he quoted from Henry James' essay 'The art of fiction': 'Try to be one of those on whom nothing is lost.' The curse of the artist: all sensors and no armour.

When people talk about writing the advice usually is to write about what you know. This is usually taken to mean that if you're a bank manager, write about being a bank manager. What it actually means is write about what you know emotionally because then you begin to discover that you know more than you thought you knew about the world. Some of what we know seems so obvious we assume everybody else knows the same. Not always true. A decent novelist will work out those insights he or she shares and those he or she doesn't and use them accordingly.

Deborah felt the *Whales* novel – the adaptation of the screenplay – had problems. We met a couple of times to discuss it and although it was never explicitly stated, it was clear she didn't think it passed muster. The problem seemed to be that it was too plot-driven. Novels need to be built organically. *Whales* wasn't. Deborah made some recommendations but having written seven drafts of the film script and seventy thousand words of the novel I have come to hate all of the characters in it and they seem to hate me. We can't spend any more time together so – for the time being at least – I'm out.

This is the second novel since *Minding* I've junked. I wrote a hundred-and-fifty pages of a novel called *Human Resources*, a follow-up to my BBC novel, *The Silent Sentry* ('Richly textured' the *Independent*). Deborah decided that it wasn't the thing I should be doing. I needed to move on. So nearly three years of writing down the pan. The problem is I know she's right. She is always right which is unquestionably the reason she's been responsible for more writers than any other agent to stand blinking under the lights on Booker Prize night accepting their plaudits. *Whales* is OK but not good enough. *Human Resources* is amusing – but so what? I need to write something that says something new, or something old in a new way; something relevant; something that develops organically; something that *needs* to be written – and very little actually does.

Much of learning to be a writer is, I suppose, discerning those reasons, developing the muscle of objectivity. When you begin you write to scratch the itch. It feels like a passing compulsion. But for some it won't go away. You can't not write because it has become as important to you as breathing. Once that happens you've had it. Published or not, you're trapped. But then perhaps you begin to ask yourself questions about why this compulsion is there. Writing is a dialogue with yourself. Forget the plaudits (there aren't many), forget wearing *writer* as a badge (useless vanity), forget the huge financial returns (unlikely): instead, examine the purpose of that dialogue. What are you telling yourself, and how might that have a more universal relevance? You won't be taught that on a creative writing course but it's the only thing worth knowing. But be careful. Speak to those close to writers. You'll learn that their addiction can be harmful to others. You can't be in two places at once, and, while writing, you can be cut off from the people closest to you. As Rilke cautioned, don't embark on this journey without giving it serious consideration.

'Ask yourself in the most silent hour of your night: must I write? Dig into yourself for a deep answer. And if this answer rings out in assent, if you meet this solemn question with a strong, simple "I must," then build your life in accordance with this necessity; your whole life, even into its humblest and most indifferent hour, must become a sign and witness to this impulse. Then come close to Nature. Then, as if no one had ever tried before, try to say what you see and feel and love and lose . . .'

So, to that end, I've started something else. I think it's going to be called *Nimrod's Shadow* and it feels right. *Publishing rule 11: When a book is harder not to write than to write you're forced to start it.* For me (and I assume other novelists) when a new story arrives it invades all the senses: a taste, even a smell, a colour or hue, rarely a phrase or the image of a character, never an opening line. *Nimrod's Shadow* came as the smell of a damp alley in North London, the taste of coal smoke on the palate. For a moment I was there with a painter and his dog.

I put words down and the painter, Reilly, and his dog, Nimrod, emerged from the fog, and then I began to follow them as they went about their lives, Nimrod leading the way. That was key, that small detail. Nearly forty thousand words done so probably about halfway through. I couldn't bear for this one to end up in the bin but have to face the prospect that it might. Perhaps Deborah is trying to tell me something by gently refusing to send my latest efforts out. I wonder how I would feel if I was never published again.

Nimrod's Shadow has a dual plot. It begins in 1912 with the story of T. F. Reilly – an obsessive painter in egg tempera who lives with his dog, Nimrod, in a garret in Old Cross (somewhere in North London, probably Camden). His only friend, Mountjoy, has convinced him to hold an exhibition of his work and has volunteered his coffee shop (the 1912 equivalent of a café) as the venue. Something dreadful happens on the day of the exhibition. The result is that Reilly, as an artist, remains obscure and on the wrong side of the law. This is weaved together with another strand – this one is contemporary and features a woman who comes across one of Reilly's pictures in a gallery. She falls in love with it and becomes obsessed with him, spending all of her time trying to discover what happened to him and his work. Obscure, frustrated artist works in garret. Another autobiographical piece.

Incidentally, the TV company which was very excited about *Minding* has gone silent too, although I did meet a young producer at another TV company to discuss *Ivan*. I pitched an idea about a middle-aged couple taking a gap year and she seemed interested. I've sent her a treatment and await the call.

I've now been paid for *Minding*, the option on the TV script, the short story for the *Express* (this took six months to come through), and the piece I did on Raymond Carver for the *Indy* (also just arrived). So the accounts for the year now show a hefty profit of nearly £2000. However, I've just found a £845 Corporation Tax bill in my folder from last year's accounts which has to be paid in October so I can't blow it all. I process the writing income through a company. It seemed like a good idea until Gordon closed all the tax loopholes and my novels stopped earning unrealistic advances. I still like the notion of being a company director but wonder if paying nearly 50 per cent of my earnings for that privilege is worth it.

Rereading this I see the phrase 'cease to exist' when writers disappear from the newspaper columns. Mmm. Probably shouldn't examine that any more closely.

7th November

Another entry. More displacement activity than anything. *Nimrod* was progressing rapidly – another four or five thousand words in less than a week, but it has stalled and I now approach it tentatively wondering if it has died or is just resting. I've been talking about it too much and if you do that novels have a habit of getting their own back by sulking. *Publishing rule 12: Novels can be 'talked out'. What happens is that while you're enthusing about the work in progress your brain decides it must be finished so starts to apply itself elsewhere. When you return to it the folder in your mind has become corrupted and the thing is dead. You can appeal and occasionally if you're incredibly contrite your subconscious will allow you to continue with it, but not always.* With my works in progress I always get stuck around pages sixty-six and a hundred-and-thirty. I don't know why but I'm always stalled for a while at both of those points – the pieces I've junked are either of those lengths.

In *Nimrod*, the 1912 protagonist, Reilly, is in jail (as I had planned), and the protagonist in the contemporary storyline (Samantha Dodd – always referred to in full) is, I think, going insane which I had not planned. Quite a considerable number of my characters end up this way (sorry, slightly John Major-ish sentence – it just came out that way). I'm not sure how advisable this is but part of the process of writing is allowing the characters to dictate their own destinies. Obviously you as the author have influence over this, but not the entire responsibility, not if the characters are alive. I tried to end my first published novel (*After the Raid*: the story of a man fleeing London haunted by the horrors of the blitz – 'Haunting, intense and enviably accomplished' Nick Hornby) on a note of hope. It wouldn't work. The characters would not be coerced into a happy ending. But now I'm somewhere around the mid-point of *Nimrod* I remind myself to trust the process. Any novelist will recognise this. It's the mystical connection between you and the plot and the characters. The process kicks in five or ten minutes (if you're lucky) after you sit down at the keyboard and open the file. Sometimes it lasts only a few minutes. On rare days it lasts two or three hours. Occasionally it doesn't kick in at all and that's when the fear takes hold. If this happens, chances are you've taken yourself down a blind alley and you have to haul the narrative back a few pages. It's usually a plot rather than character issue. If your protagonists are real enough they'll allow you to do this, unless they're sulking. If they are then you're in trouble.

I'm still writing on the train journey home. Most of my novels have been written on the train to and from the day job (see accounts for reason). Increasingly difficult to concentrate with mobile phone conversations going on around me. Two nights ago a man opposite (lean cycling type – lycra, sweaty, tortured) phoned his girlfriend to discuss visiting Lewes on bonfire night. He made the mistake of asking if they were meeting anybody there. A pause. Then:

'. . . No. That would be great . . . No, not at all . . . of course. . . ye . . . yes, it'll be good for just the two of us to do something together for a change . . .'

This went on for about twenty minutes. Poor sod.

Last week Posy Simmonds was one of the guests on *Midweek*. Libby asked her how she went about getting the dialogue of her characters. Some of it came from over-hearing mobile phone calls: 'People are so kind,' she said with a Posy Simmonds-ish smile on her face, 'they talk so loudly.'

8th November

1.35 p.m. Day off from work so attempting to write. Instead, more displacement activity: leaf sweeping, four cups of tea, one decaf coffee, two digestives, one chocolate biscuit, one banana, tuna sandwich, five minutes of *Loose Women* on TV, trip to Asda, writing this, making the evening meal, up and down the bloody stairs time after time after time, trooping around the house, dog's eyes following me. Should walk her. Two hundred words and Reilly still stuck in prison. Feel like I'm in there with him. Trying to get the period details right. He's still in Pentonville. 1912. I wanted him to be in Millbank on remand but discover it had been demolished by then. Pentonville will have to do. Nice detail I dug up of them bringing the gallows' beam and other hanging paraphernalia from Newgate when they demolished that prison. If he is hanged I might use that if it fits, though it probably won't.

Also found out that Pentonville was used to run week-long courses for hangmen. Another interesting detail. Apparently they practised on a dummy, learning the knots, the length of drop etc. Condemned men were routinely weighed. They assumed an interest in their welfare, the truth was it was solely to do with calculating the right drop. The watchword was speed and precision: put on the white hood, pull out the safety pin, pull the lever, and drop! Pierrepoint prided himself on twenty seconds from the moment the prisoner reached the gallows to the drop. I think thirteen seconds was his record. The victim is then left dangling for an hour. The superstar hangman at the time was John Ellis, a barber from Rochdale. He returned to cutting hair between jobs. Ellis hanged Crippen and it earned him notoriety. People used to come and sit in his barber's shop just to see the man who'd despatched the mass murderer. The trickiest ones to hang were apparently the ones who'd tried to kill themselves by cutting their throats. Presumably there was an extra training module at Pentonville (optional) on that one. Ellis seemed to cope well with his profession until, one day, he tried to shoot himself. Sadly for him, he missed and was only wounded. Suicide being a crime at the time he was tried and found guilty. It wasn't, however, a hanging offence so he was spared the irony of a death on the gallows for trying and failing to top himself.

The trick in a novel is to use just enough period detail without overlarding it. Big crime. *Publishing rule 13: Rule of thumb by this non-prizewinning novelist is not to use any detail in a period novel you wouldn't include in a contemporary novel.* So don't bang on about the LGOC B-type bus (introduced in 1910) unless it's germane to the plot. However, it's permissible to mention that Mountjoy (a secondary character) climbs the open staircase to the top deck. The open staircase is enough to suggest he's not on a bendy-bus or a Routemaster. Philip Roth is unquestionably a great writer but he's guilty of information overload. He must have done some serious research into the history of glove making because in *American Pastoral* there are pages of extraneous detail. Ditto Ian McEwan and the brain operation in one of his recent efforts (*Saturday*, I think).

Every piece of information is a trigger and as a writer you need to know what you're triggering: sometimes you're just signposting something, sometimes suggesting emotion, sometimes telegraphing a plot point. The most effective passages are those that do all three. A recent review in the *TLS* made the observation that the writer was a 'good reader of his own work'. I hadn't thought about that until I read it – but that's what you need to be, or need to learn to be – a reader of exactly how your cues are being picked up by the reader. Easy to do the first or second time you read through – increasingly hard as time goes on. By the time you've finished writing the thing you might have read a page eighty, ninety or even more times ('The first draft of anything is shit' Ernest Hemingway).

When writing period novels the other useful trick is to read novels set in the period. Not so much for detail but for the taste and flavour.

Chicken stock needs turning off. Are you supposed to leave the bones and stuff in the pan while it cools? Don't know. I'll look it up. Tasted a bit bland half an hour ago – I hope it perks up a bit.

Displacement activity is of course important. The novel is in your brain, processing away, day and night, whatever you're doing. The hope is that when you get back to it it will feel easier. You must learn to access the folder in which the processing is being done, otherwise it's wasted. The unconscious mind is the writer's best friend. As Ray Bradbury put it, 'Your intuition knows what to write, so get out of the way.'

Can't find any info. on whether bones should be left in or out the stock. Think I'll leave them in and walk the dog so we'll probably all die of botulism later tonight. No. Dog later. Get back to Reilly in Pentonville, sketching his cell in charcoal (would he have been allowed a sketchpad and charcoal? Possibly. He's on remand so will have been allowed his own clothes, visits from solicitor, writing letters and extra food if he has the money to buy it.) 13.45. Ten minutes wasted. One more pointless email to Fay to ask if there have been any developments on the *Cockroach* project then back to Reilly. Must close this file now. Just reread this entry then close it. OK. That's it. Back to Reilly.

9th November

Just a quickie picking up from the 8th Nov. entry about extraneous historical detail. In today's *TLS* Mark Kamine takes Elmore Leonard to task for his pedantry in his new novel. It's something most writers are guilty of and the observation is a useful one. Leonard's piece is, he suggests, 'loaded with exposition, as if Leonard were more worried about his readers' lack of familiarity with its era than about his characters' believability. "The Battle of the Bulge was Germany's last full-out assault," one character tells another. "They pushed off the sixteenth of December with a thousand tanks and by the twentieth of January they had a hundred thousand casualties and lost eight hundred of the tanks." This in a conversation occurring in April 1945, a few months after the events discussed.'

Realised as I wrote this that I am engaged in more displacement activity. The more entries in the journal the worse the novel is going. Fingers crossed for no more entries for a while.

11th November

A moving TV programme by Jeremy Paxman on Wilfred Owen marking Armistice Day. Interesting on the issue of writerly collaboration. Paxo went down to the vaults in the British Museum (twenty metres beneath the Euston Road) with an eager young archivist. Wearing white gloves he tugged out two volumes of Owen's original manuscripts. In the reworkings you can see how much influence Sassoon had on his young protégé. They encountered each other, of course, in a hospital in 1918. Sassoon had been sent there because he'd been writing anti-war letters to the papers. Owen was there because of shell shock. When they met Owen's poetry was unlocked. Interesting that in some lines he offers Sassoon two bracketed word options and Sassoon deletes the one he likes least. 'Anthem for Doomed Youth' was given its final title by Sassoon. Owen's first stab was 'Anthem for Dead Youth' – but dead is crossed out and doomed inserted above it. Much stronger, much more eternal. Be interesting to see other examples of discarded titles: I'm sure Radio 4 could construct a whole new radio series out of them. It would be billed as 'a sideways look at . . .', radio shorthand for a particular type of broadcasting humour – no laughs, just pinched half gasps from the aged audience, rather like death rattles. I remember the DJ Dave Lee Travis doing a similar thing on Radio 1 decades ago. He encouraged listeners to write in (they didn't have text or email then and young people could still write more than a sentence without exhausting themselves – or their vocabulary) with suggestions for prequels to well-known novels. The Hairy Cornflake then read them out. The only one I remember is 'The Eagle Has Just Taken Off' which I remember thinking hilarious at the time.

Come to think of it, 'A sideways look . . .' could well work as the new sherry-hour TV quiz format, hosted by grannies' favourite Xander Armstrong. The premise is simple – things (animate and inanimate) photographed from side on. Contestants have to identify them until 'sadly' one is eliminated. I might write it up and offer it to the BBC's fact controller, Richard Osman.

Interesting how close to tears Paxman allows himself to be exposed on TV when he's not on *Newsnight* (he did one of those programmes about his family history a while back and wept openly). A new man. He seems to have gone through it and increasingly wears his pain etched round his eyes.

Yesterday John Mortimer was on the radio talking about writing. He was asked if he ever used music to help him write. He said he didn't because he needed to hear the music of the sentences in his head. It's assumed that poets do this but few understand how much effort goes into creating prose rhythms, planing sentences down again and again until they run smoothly. Paxo finished the programme by telling us that Owen's mother received the telegram informing her of her beloved son's death on Armistice Day – the crowds outside her front door cheering in celebration of the cessation of hostilities.

13th November

Emailed Fay again today to ask about progress on *Cockroach*. Obviously there hasn't been any news otherwise she'd already have been on the phone – or possibly arrived in person in a chauffeur-driven Rolls Royce to deliver it. However, such calls are important to keep the client prominent in the agent's consciousness (that, at least, is this client's view though probably not one shared by his agent). Couple of 'nice rejection letters' apparently. *Publishing rule 14: One of the tricks agents learn early on is not to contact the writer when such rejections come through. What's the point, after all, of calling to say somebody has turned down your project? Instead they're saved and delivered to the writer when he or she calls for an update. This serves the dual purpose of demonstrating to the writer that the agent has been busy on his behalf and it also sugars the pill of the silence on the current project. The nasty rejections are presumably deleted.*

Fay is holding off sending the new thing to any more companies in the States due to the current strike by the all-powerful Writer's Guild of America (WGA). Jay Leno reportedly handed out doughnuts to strikers on the picket line outside NBC's Burbank Studio. 'Without them I'm not funny,' he said to reporters. 'I'm a dead man.' The dispute is over DVD residuals and residuals on shows streamed via the net. The last time they struck in 1988 it cost Hollywood $500m and the regional economy possibly double that (the entertainment industry is southern California's biggest earner, worth $30bn) so pressure is on for a rapid resolution. The WGA is asking for 2.5 cents in the $ on internet revenues. The *Guardian* estimates these to be worth $4.6bn over the next three years and points out how important residuals are to writers, quoting the case of Marc Cherry, the man behind *The Golden Girls*. The show ran until 1992 but he then struggled through a twelve-year drought, living off residuals, until he came back with *Desperate Housewives*. One reporter visited the picket lines and said he'd never seen as many Porsches and Audis in the studio lots. Arnold Schwarzenegger is now involved and hopes to use his muscle to bring the dispute to a rapid conclusion.

Interesting to see what would happen if the British novelists went on strike for a fairer deal (subsidised heating bills, haemorrhoid remedies or a slipper allowance, for example). I doubt anybody would notice for a couple of years. Agents and publishers would probably welcome it as it would cut their workload and the number of whining phone calls they have to take on a daily basis – the cost to the publishing industry about £25 and a couple of expense account lunches.

A few years ago I was involved with a group of writers who met on a monthly basis in a dismal chilly room above a dire West London pub. We were all published, among us some fairly well-established (if senior) names. I went along expecting sparkling conversation and came away depressed by the litany of whingeing over advances, agents, television people, the lack of interest from the film industry etc. (yes indeed – the subject matter of this journal). One elderly woman novelist always spent the evening complaining she couldn't get decent typewriter ribbons nowadays. This always provoked the anti-computer chorus: the techno-phobes who all seemed to write on old Amstrad computers and couldn't work out why they kept losing their works in progress when the things crashed. The saddest thing to witness (apart from the charity shop clothing) was the way in which these impoverished individuals scuttled to the bar on their way in, careful not to meet anybody's eye, then pretended to notice the group only as they brought over their cheap glass of house red wine (large) which they would then nurse for the next three hours. Nobody took the risk of going to the bar in case they had to buy a round. Anybody who did strike gold tended to come to one fur-ther meeting to brag about it, then disappear (presumably to Hollywood to join the WGA) never to be seen again. One notable and rare success story was a female novelist who began publishing roughly at the same time that I did, and for a while we shared a similar low-flying career tra-jectory. Her luck changed when Hollywood optioned a novel. One night she took a phone call from a Hollywood mogul who announced to her as she picked up the phone: 'I'm going to make you a very rich woman.' And he did. The man was Harvey Weinstein.

At 10.30 p.m. there was a mass exodus to the tubes to the far reaches of the capital or the unfashionable resorts of the south coast (many seemed to live in Hastings). I may re-join if they haven't all perished from hypothermia.

Needless to say, *Nimrod's Shadow* is still stalled although there is light at the end of the current tunnel. Managed to grind out two hundred words this morning and will see if there's more to be done now. One of the oddest things about novels is that when you've finished them and read them back it's very hard to spot the passages you've had to force out among those that have come more easily. Novel writing is continuity of expression. I have 26 per cent of my battery remaining so will attempt to use it to good effect. Meeting agent Deborah for lunch on Friday and have an early meeting with the company I sent the TV treatment to.

18th November

Yesterday a write-off (note to self: *A Write Off*, possible alternative title for this book). Early meeting with TV company cancelled – producer stuck on a train which didn't move for two hours due to a person on the line. Cancelled lunch with agent Deborah due to her appalling cough. She bravely said she was happy to meet but seemed relieved when I suggested postponing it 'til Monday. She reported that her husband said it was like sleeping with a walrus and was still coughing when she put the phone down. Emailed Fay to tell her about the cancelled TV meeting but got an 'out of office' reply saying she wouldn't be back until Monday. On the positive side a cheque arrived from the Revenue for early payment of Corporation Tax: £1.72. Not sure what to squander it on.

News in the papers that Amazon is about to launch the book equivalent of an iPod – a 'Kindle'. Readers will be able to pay for downloads of books on to a palm-sized screen which means they'll never have to buy another book. Inevitably this means that book sales will further fall, pirate copies will be available on the net, and returns to authors will further decline.

27th November

Finally meet up with Deborah for lunch. She despairs of bookshops nowadays, she says. She doesn't recognise anything about them. As always we had a good, low-key lunch. I'd sent her thirty-odd pages of *Nimrod's Shadow* and she was cagey about it. Found it tonally uneven at the start so will go back to it. She asks when she can see more but I'm loath to send any more until it's done. Representing many of the literary superstars of the country, indeed world, I'm amazed that she continues to encourage and support me. Her philosophy is that it's a combination of luck, talent and hitting the zeitgeist that propels you ahead of the pack. Needless to say, *Nimrod* is still edging forward at a snail's pace. We discussed the last novel, *Minding*, and she said I was lucky, at least I'd had some reviews. There were good novels being published that got absolutely none. We talked about a writer she represented and she described him as 'the real thing'. I know what she means, and obviously so does she, but I was too afraid to ask if she felt the same way about me.

I was introduced to Deborah by a colleague at the BBC. After giving up on writing radio plays (one transmitted as a *Thirty Minute Theatre* on Radio 4, many subsequently rejected – see appendix), I wrote a novel and she read it for me. She thought it had merit and said she'd give it to her friend. A couple of months later I got a letter from Deborah inviting me to come and meet her. Only when I walked into her agency did I realise how significant she was. Her room was exactly what you'd hope an agent's office to be – tall bookshelves filled chaotically with several thousand hardbacks, manuscripts stacked on the floor, dim lighting, a couple of old sofas, one of which was covered with manuscripts, and a cluttered desk. We got on immediately. She told me that she was no longer taking on clients but she'd decided to make an exception for me. The novel (*Deserters*, the story of the relationships of a troubled ex-army drifter set largely in Brighton) went out to a few publishers but there were no bites. I wrote another, *Draper's Gazette* (about an elderly local newspaper reporter), but she didn't consider it strong enough to send out and encouraged me to try again. In parallel with that one I'd been tinkering with a novel set in the London blitz. I'd been back to it on numerous occasions having started it a couple of years before but was stuck at page sixty-six. Each time I returned to it I knew it was worth finishing. Finally I broke through, finished it, and sent it off. Deborah summoned me by phone a couple of weeks later. I waited in the agency reception chatting to the receptionist. Deborah opened her door with a huge smile on her face, holding my manuscript under her arm. 'I can sell this,' she said. Within three weeks we had an offer from Jonathan Cape. Nothing in my career will ever match the moment Deborah appeared from her office.

I spoke to Fay a couple of days ago about the screenplays. The young director who described an earlier screenplay as 'stupendous' thanked her for sending him the new one but apologises that he won't get to it yet as he's just started shooting something new. An American company she sent *Whales* to also came back to her last week. They had a good heart-to-heart, during which the producer told her he loved the script but there was no way he'd convince his company to do it as it was too expensive, so she'll send him the new one (*An American Cockroach*, based on the novel *Newton's Swing*, a novel about an Englishman transplanted to New York, the shooting dead of his wife in their apartment and the effect of the murder on him and his young son – a who- and why-dunnit) when the writer's strike is over. The companies aren't accepting anything to look at while it's still on. The Brit distribution company who were keen on *Cockroach* still haven't got back to her and she's not going to hassle them in case we look desperate – which obviously we're not.

In the post today my annual unearned statements from Random House which (who?) hold the rights to 90 per cent of my *oeuvre*. Going through each page the news gets more and more grim. For example – *After the Raid* – first novel. Under 'Current period – Home sales, export sales, and Europe sales' – Nought. Ditto *Deserters*, *Morning all Day* and *Newton's Swing* (hardback). Paperback news on *Newton's Swing* is marginally better. Although home sales were minus one (i.e., one copy returned to the warehouse over the year) there were two export sales – a net gain of one book. *The Silent Sentry* showed home sales of minus three with no export sales to balance them. *A Town by the Sea* fared even worse: minus five home sales in hardback and minus fourteen in paperback, while export sales were minus twenty-four. My total worldwide sales for this year for all titles owned by Random House (seven novels in paperback and hardback, i.e., fourteen in all) amounted to minus forty-five. I have therefore sold forty-five fewer novels than an unpublished writer. No mean feat.

Does anybody, therefore, apart from me really give a damn whether the latest novel is stalled? I mean – really?

Julie's dad for some reason owned the collected works of Charles Dickens, and she inherited them. He was a proofreader, and he died much too young at fifty-nine.

Robert Maxwell took over his company and stole his pension. I don't know why but this morning I took the copy of *The Old Curiosity Shop* from the shelf and put it in my bag. Been feeling somewhat grim over the last few days if the truth be told but reading the book on the train lifted my spirits. Something about the act of reading something really good forces you to look outside yourself. Julie is away in Rome for three days and while she's away I'll read it. Her dad stamped 'Ex Libris John Bancroft' in each book and it made me feel unutterably sad when I opened it, for him and for Julie who I know still misses him and always will.

4th December

Nimrod progressing again. A few days of creativity. Further to Deborah's comments a couple of weeks back on not recognising what she sees in bookshops any more, the *TLS* reports on a Royal Society of Literature debate at which the agent, Clare Alexander, said, 'We have the stupidest bestseller list in the world at the moment.' *The New York Times* Book Review column 'Inside the list' printed the London *Times* charts without further comment.

1. *On the Edge* Richard Hammond
2. *New Europe* Michael Palin
3. *Survivor* Sharon Osbourne
4. *Don't Stop Me Now* Jeremy Clarkson
5. *Long Way Down* Ewan McGregor and Charley Boorman

But there's no point in sneering. People don't seem to like surprises any more and even prefer their books pre-digested. All of these are, in some way, TV spin-offs in which the story is already well known. Hammond is the diminutive hack who happened to become newsworthy because he suffered a bad car crash on TV. Without the crash he wouldn't have had a book to write. But why buy the book? Who knows? Men are notoriously difficult to buy for if they don't have a hobby, and most don't, so I suppose the *Top Gear* book is marginally better than socks for a birthday present. The *Top Gear* trio are flavour of the month at the moment and they're all making the most of it. Who can blame them? Next year it will be someone else's turn and we'll be spared the sight of them giggling and grinning at each other every time we turn on the telly. But at least books are being bought and without this lot the conglomerates wouldn't have the resources to prop up their fragile literary imprints, most of which make a loss. So three cheers for Jezza Clarkson, Captain Slow and The Hamster. Incidentally, the WGA strike is still on.

20th December

Busy month at work and some progress on *Nimrod's Shadow*. Think I've pushed through the block on it and now nearly sixty thousand words in. It feels OK again.

Not much to report on the other projects. No word on *Ivan* (producer on her nuptials and no word since her return). A 'no' back from the British distribution company on *Cockroach*. No reason given but they said they'd be interested in distributing it in the unlikely event it gets made.

Two parties: one at my publishers who have moved to swish offices in Holland Park. I grandly call them 'my publishers' but as we have no contract beyond the last book they're no more mine than anybody else's – and given the recent sales figures perhaps less mine than anybody else's. Each time I write a new book, Deborah asks if I want her to try for a two-book deal. I always resist the temptation. Against the obvious benefit of having the thing pre-sold and publication guaranteed I worry I'm going to be landed with a debt I can't pay off if I don't manage to finish the thing. Very odd food at the party. Plates of boiled quails' eggs on beds of ivy served up by young people in crisp white shirts. Not really of much use to soak up the copious (and decent) red wine. Met the new editor of *Granta* who managed to sound enthusiastic when I offered to send him a new story I'd written. He reviewed my first novel in the *Indy* or the *TLS* and pretended to remember.

Also went to the Xmas party at the agent's. Deborah turned up after it had started as she always does with a huge plate of small, warm sausages fetched out from the boot of her car. Spent much of the evening as usual commiserating with other mid-listers on our paltry annual publisher's statements, moaning about the Booker shortlist, and looking enviously at the two or three mega-selling lit novelists perched on the arms of the Chesterfields, a small crowd hanging on their every word.

This year there is a large number of TV newsreaders and breakfast TV presenters in attendance. One of the agents is hoovering them up and encouraging them to render their day jobs into fictional form. Somehow, even in the dim, smoke-filled rooms of the agency, they glow. Perhaps it's fame or familiarity, or maybe they wear studio make-up when they go out.

So it looks like 2007 is over for this ailing writer. I might manage a few pages of *Nimrod* over the festive break. The table in the back bedroom feels like a nest now, to which I return with some pleasure. At my left elbow a view across the playing fields to the nearby school, ahead of me a wall, against which is propped a poster of a painting by Peter Messer, the tempera artist whose work first inspired *Nimrod*. Pile of books on the desk, *Crime and Punishment* at the top of the pile. Must get a new chair in the new year.

WGA strike still on so I can continue to use it as an excuse for *Cockroach* not to have been optioned by an American company. Here's to 2008.

2008

14th January

Alongside the festivities *Nimrod's Shadow* has been moving on. Sixty-nine thousand words now so it's already longer than most of my other novels and it doesn't seem to be reaching the end yet. I'm happy with the progress but it does feel slow. Some days writing is grunt work; a plot point has to be reached and there's nothing to do but to grind out the words (trying to make them as interesting as possible) until the point has been made. There are few joyous days when the thing just sings along. *Publishing rule 15: You can count on perhaps 10 per cent of your writing time breezing along happily – the rest is fairly grim as Thomas Mann memorably noted: 'A writer is somebody for whom writing is more difficult than it is for other people.'*

I think the problem with this one is that there are two voices – one for the 1912 story, the other for the contemporary one so each time the switch is made the voice has to be re-found.

The WGA strike is still on and has now claimed the Golden Globes which, instead of the usual glitzy red-carpet affair, were announced by a bemused man (Mexican I think) at a press conference. The event looked like it had been choreographed by the Cohen brothers. Apparently this will make the BAFTAs a much more important occasion. American stars who wouldn't usually be seen dead at this second-rate affair (hosted by Jonathan Ross) are clamouring to declare their availability.

Lunch last Friday with David from the lit. agents. David used to work as an assistant to Deborah and I've known him for years. He's now an agent in his own right. Decent pub lunch, several pints of Staropramen, usual moans about the industry. He brought along a grubby plastic carrier bag of proofs and manuscripts from the office for my perusal (suspect he fished them out of his recycling bin on the way out as they were all dog-eared and one of the proofs looked suspiciously like it had teabag residue on it). Nice-looking biography of Conrad in there which he midwifed. Loyally he asked how the new book was going. I told him, though confessed that I suspected there were few people waiting with bated breath for its delivery. He thought for a moment and then said, 'Well I'm sure there are three or four.' Not quite the reassurance I'd been hoping for but an honest assessment of my literary stock. He asked to read a bit of it so I emailed off thirty pages.

Googled myself over Xmas (only once) and found a heartening comment on one of the *Guardian* books forums. Contributors had been asked for their book of the year and somebody chose *Minding*, adding that she couldn't work out why nobody had heard of me. Perhaps, she suggested, it was because I operated beneath the literary radar: a literary stealth bomber. I like that and might use it in future publicity: 'A literary stealth bomber' the *Guardian*.

For some reason I decided to email the screenplay of *Thought About You* to the promising young director I worked with on the failed *Whales* project. Fairly pointless really as he hadn't responded to the increasingly pained and petty emails I sent. Anyway, rather than leaving it languishing on the hard drive of the PC I thought it was worth a try. He emailed back almost immediately to say he'd been thinking about me and looked forward to reading it. Also wished me a Happy New Year and signed off, 'Hope we can get something made soon.' Indeed. Needless to say no communication from him since.

Been asked by a friend of ours to go to her book group, at which they will be discussing *Minding*. Said I would. At least it will shift five or six copies and it's always interesting to hear opinions on your work from people who have troubled to read it closely. That's in a month's time.

Book came through the post yesterday from *Granta* magazine. The third and final volume of Simon Gray's *Smoking Diaries*. It seems he remembered a conversation we had at the *Granta* Xmas party, which is more than I did until now. It wasn't much of a conversation – more me saying quite drunkenly how much I admired his writing and him (soberly and graciously – he's now permanently off the booze) thanking me and clearly wondering who the hell I was. He must subsequently have found out, though how I don't know as there were probably only three or four people in the room who knew who I was, including me – obviously, but even I was unsure by then – so only two or three. Anyway, then somebody more important was steered in front of him and I left them to it. But I do admire him and can't understand why he's not lauded to the rafters. Better than Pinter in my opinion; without Samuel Beckett, Pinter wouldn't have had a voice to use.

The encounter with Simon Gray reminds me of the first time I went to a Christmas party at my agent's. Terrified, I fortified myself on the way there and at some point in the evening stumbled up to Ian McEwan, burbling on about how he was the reason I started writing. I still wince when I remember. This wasn't flannel, but what an idiot. McEwan looked kindly (soberly and graciously) back and said, 'No, you're the reason you started writing.' Which of course was a typically cool McEwan-ish type of statement. On my way out Kazuo Ishiguro ('Ish' as he's known in the trade) asked if I wanted a lift back to the station in his Volvo. I thanked him but declined, feeling somewhat queasy. Didn't want to kick off my brilliant career by blowing my chunks in the back of Ish's new estate.

Literary parties were different then. Using the toilet (is it toilet, lavatory or washroom in polite society nowadays?) always posed problems as there would usually be a poet unconscious or asleep in there. People nowadays don't drink as much. Which reminds me (I'm aware I'm beginning to sound like Ronnie Corbett) of a party at the BBC in which a friend of mine, very pissed, saw Alan Yentob in the Gents, staggered up to him and said 'Yentob by name, Yentob by nature,' then staggered away again. And while we're on the subject of lavatorial encounters it also reminds me of once following one of Britain's leading playwrights into a BBC lavatory. He was giving a talk to the staff about his latest lush TV epic. Throughout the evening he'd been twirling a bent red drinking straw between the thumb and first finger of his right hand.

I stood beside him at the urinals and was amazed to see that even as he pissed he continued to twiddle the straw, todger (presumably – I didn't look down) in his left hand.

Yesterday got my annual statement through from PLR (Public Lending Right, i.e., the commission authors are paid on library lendings): £138. Not bad. Had I been writing full time it would have paid last month's phone bill.

Minding's Amazon sales rank, incidentally, is now 342,000.

21st January

Trying to write on the train this morning but was interrupted by the guttural bray of the man sitting in the seat across the aisle. He's a regular on the train, his accent hard to place. It sits somewhere between Irish and South African, and when he uses his mobile he shouts – not just the pitched-too-loud disinhibited volume that most mobile users adopt, but a full-voiced shout. This drew a few weary glances from the commuters sitting around him, but as the conversation progressed (something about the attitude of one of his employees being unacceptable and 'IT'S NOT GOOD ENOUGH' for some reason) people started laughing. One wag at the end of the carriage started answering his questions, eliciting further guffaws. Needless to say this has destroyed my fragile concentration so work on *Nimrod* will have to wait for tonight. A couple more thousand words on. Another lull but it's edging forward. Verdict has been passed on Reilly.

Recession is biting according to the news this morning. Record stock market crashes. Interesting signifier of this in the train is the increasing number of commuters (including me) bringing midget thermos flasks with them to save the daily £1.80 on their morning tall latte. Looking round I can see six other tiny aluminium chimneys on the tables. Last year there was only one. For some reason thermos flasks always look retro – they wouldn't seem out of place in *Lost in Space*. Like bringing sandwiches to work or being a naturist, they always used to be considered a signal of eccentricity, possibly also mental illness. Not so now. Problem is that tea stored in them is almost undrinkable – takes on a metallic tint. Coffee is just about acceptable. I drink only decaf now. This was prompted by reading an interview with John Banville after he won the Booker for *The Sea* (I reviewed the book for the *Literary Review* – who, incidentally pay £28 for what must amount to two or three days' work) and for once agreed with the judges' choice. Anyway, he said he'd given up proper coffee because it made him feel terribly bleak. He could actually trace these feelings to the coffee. It set me to wondering if I had the same affliction – feeling somewhat desperate by mid-morning on a daily basis. I gave up caffeinated coffee and hey presto, no more morning misery. (Well, not as much as before.)

The upside to giving up on the novel this morning is that (when I've finished this) I can return guilt-free to Simon Gray's diaries, which are brilliant. As the volumes have progressed he's written more about the details of his daily life and less about his past. Volume three consists almost entirely of observations he makes over the rims of his specs while he's writing his journals. Almost as if he sits down to write, gets up, lives a bit, sits down, writes another couple of lines, i.e., the process of the writing has become his subject matter. There's something compelling about sharing someone else's consciousness for a while, especially that of someone like Simon Gray. Makes you realise that we all experience similar terrors and sense of isolation, just process them in different ways. Charles Bukowski picked up on this in his autobiographical novel *Ham on Rye*. 'When someone else's truth is the same as your truth, and he seems to be saying it just for you, that's great.' Absurd, though, to comment further. Journal entries about another writer's journal entries about writing a journal probably an uncommercial new literary genre.

This is what I can hear in the carriage and why writing today is therefore impossible:

'. . . agree to what I want and see if that works that way . . . no I . . . who? Sorry, is this? . . . Yeah . . . there are . . . at least we can go. Look, I'll speak to you this afternoon. Yeah.'

'Good morning it's Darren, how can I help you? . . . You called me. How can I help? . . . [long pause].

'. . . Next stop East Croydon. This is coach number one . . . of eight.'

'. . . Right . . . right. Sorry I'm on a train so I'm losing my signal . . . right, so you want me to find out if there's a transcript of the first interview . . . or, so is the . . . second interview? Yueeeear. . . right . . . mmm . . . Oh . . . OK I will, I'll email my solicitor now and see if I can get a reply. Yeah. Thanks. Bye.'

'Ladies and gentlemen, the next station will be East Croydon . . . Change here for stations to London Bridge and Pancras International. Thank you.'

[Sound effect] Train horn.

Small wonder *Nimrod* is progressing slowly.

The WGA strike, by the way, seems almost to have been resolved. Continuing silence from Fay so no progress on the scripts. Woke up just after three the other morning with an idea for a TV drama series. It's about a man who is sent out by his wife to buy a tin of alphabetti spaghetti from the new local superstore for their supper. When he gets there the vast car park is empty bar one other man in a VW microbus, observing the huge store through binoculars. A lunatic survivalist. Suggests the man doesn't go in without chopper support. Eventually the courtesy bus arrives but the driver has used up his allocated hours so has to take a break. The man naps. Long and the short of it is that it takes him six hours to reach the doors of the eerily abandoned superstore. He goes in. The story begins. As I say, I found this in my mental inbox at 3 a.m. The pitch would be something along the lines of *Supermarket Sweep* meets *The Prisoner*. I've done about a third of an hour-long episode but have put it aside as it's just another distraction from the novel.

Incidentally, slightly testy email back from the TV company who wanted to see *Ivan*. This was as a response to three emails and one telephone call from me following our two initial (and positive) meetings. Email suggests no news on *Ivan* as the company is busy 'in production'. This, despite the producer I met in December assuring me they would read and respond to the script 'soon'. I fear another failed project. In my day job I make a point of responding quickly to all emails (however ludicrous). People deserve a line or two and it takes, what, twenty seconds?

Nearly at Victoria so another journey wasted. Will have to return to Simon Gray's diaries tonight, unless I can face *Nimrod* (a dog, you might remember, who is currently on a taxidermist's bench having his skin removed).

Minding now at Amazon sales rank 431,000.

24th January

In the light of the above, can't resist quoting something else from Simon Gray's journals which suggest it's not only mid-list writers who get treated with complete disdain. His play, *Butley*, is in rehearsal in New York. It's being revived forty years on but the actor playing a key, albeit minor, role can't get his English accent right. Gray is Blackberry'ed on holiday in Greece and asked if he'd mind rewriting the part so the popular young American actor can play the part as an American instead of an Englishman. Gray wearily agrees. However, the rewrite involves structural changes to the rest of the play – the new nationality has consequences. Victoria, his partner, duly sends off the rewrite (she has control of the Blackberry as Gray's fingers are too big for the delicate keys – besides which he seems to quite like the role Victoria plays in organising his writing life). An email comes back from New York informing him that the other actors are deeply unhappy with the rewrite as they have now to learn new lines – and, miraculously, the actor who was struggling with his accent has now overcome his block. Problem solved. Cue some righteous anger from Gray. When I got into work, I looked him up in our 'Forward Planning Database' intending to secure him for an appearance on *Midweek* when the book comes out, only to read that he's doing no publicity. He's too unwell to come to the studio. I will approach the book with caution now, looking for signs of his decline.

Newspapers report that A. L. Kennedy has won the Costa Award for her book about a Second World War pilot. The *Telegraph* reports this as 'Author and stand-up comic A. L. Kennedy', which the press now insist on labelling her. The *Telegraph* also feels obliged to add that she has suffered from depression. Why? In a four-line report wouldn't it have been more useful to mention something about the contents of the book? And wouldn't it have been more newsworthy if she hadn't suffered from depression? Most writers I know have, at some point, struggled with it. But nowadays the press wants only one story – and that's a human-interest one. 'If it bleeds it leads' remains the editor's maxim.

Email from Fay who says she's had nothing back from the British company but has put me up for a writing job on *Robinson Crusoe* for NBC – and a 'script polish' on a comedy. I do admire her tenacity but there's not a snowball's chance in hell of either. Emailed her back to tell her I'd had it with all of them and was retreating to the calm waters of literary fiction, which is where I should now be rather than writing this.

More displacement activity as *Nimrod* is at a crucial point and I know I have to address a major issue facing the main protagonist. He's getting away from me a bit, stepping into the fog, and I need to haul him back in front of the reader otherwise the last quarter of the book will fail. It feels as though the process of the court case he's facing (the legal process gives any book an off-the-peg narrative) now overshadows the character development. I have no problems with how I've represented the court, but am slightly less convinced by Reilly's reactions to what's going on around him. It's quite hard to keep saying something fresh about a man locked up alone in a cell without stating the obvious. I will return to it today.

25th January

A coda to yesterday's communication with Fay. She emails that she's beginning to despair of the industry. She may retire and write a cookbook. However, she's been thinking about *Ivan* and has decided to send it off to some young producers 'untainted by the industry' who, if they like it, might take it on and might actually make it. This is definitely a low-financial-return venture (they haven't got any money) but at least it might stand a chance of getting made with some enthusiasm and energy. Why not? I asked her to send the screenplay-length version rather than the sixty-minute version of it I did for the BBC.

Skulking around WHSmith waiting for the train I was dismayed to see that the 'leading British writer at the peak of his powers' with whom I'm sharing a platform at the Bath Lit. Festival has been chosen for the Richard & Judy Bookclub. He's now at number twenty-one in the WHS top thirty. This has, of course, elevated him way above my level so the audience will have even less interest in what I'll have to say than they would have had before.

And just before I get back to *Nimrod*, an incident on the train to report. Man across the aisle from me on the left (facing front) gets up at Haywards Heath to allow a new passenger into the vacant window seat. Aisle man has been on his laptop since Brighton and has lowered the arm separating the seats so he can rest his left elbow on it while typing. Because of the height of the carriage tables it's physically impossible to type without using such a support. When new man is settled, aisle man puts down the arm and is just about to continue typing when Mr Haywards Heath says, 'I'd rather have that up.'

'What?'

'The arm. I'd prefer to have it up.'

Pause. Glower. Aisle man relents. Mr H. H. gets out his paper. Which one had the greater right? Discuss. I'm of course in aisle man's camp and feel a disproportionate rage towards Mr H. H. with his cheap grey suit. Aisle man I feel an affinity with – a younger T-shirted chap with longish hair I've heard wishing goodnight to his young daughter on the phone on the evening train home. Commuting is a sad life sometimes. Reminds me of the death of a commuter I witnessed just as we pulled into Clapham Common station one winter's night a couple of years ago. He passed away on the train (the 19.06 semi-fast I think). Heart attack. He was surrounded by his cache of high-octane lager and daily bag of salted nuts. He went down, clutching his chest in a flurry of nuts, scattering the tins like skittles. The opened one lurched eccentrically down the aisle, spitting white foam every-where. The rest of the carriage looked on, seeing their own fates played out and mentally clocking how late this was going to make the train. Thankfully there were two doctors on the train (tip: if you're considering commuting and are in poor health, move to Brighton – there is always at least one doctor and one nurse on the train). Anyway, the train was held up until the paramedics arrived and the body of the poor sod was taken away. Some months later I wrote a story about it – 'Brian Something' – which *Punch* published. Julie says I process everything through my writing. How else can you do it without cooking a tumour?

It's now evening and I'm on my way home. Conclusion to the laptop-rage incident which I couldn't report at the time as I was getting off the train: Mr Haywards Heath resumed badgering aisle man as they were about to get off the train. Puce-faced, he said, 'I asked you, TWICE, to lift the arm of the seat.' Aisle man said he had his iPod headphones on so didn't hear – but he nevertheless offered a polite apology and let Mr Haywards Heath out into the aisle, allowing him off the train before him, thereby winning the exchange. Mr Haywards Heath will go the way of Mr Clapham Common if he's not careful.

Get to work and open the *Mail* to find the headline 'Factory fumes "made top author write pulp novels".' This was the story of Joan Brady, the first woman to be awarded the Whitbread Prize, winning a settlement of £115,000 after claiming to have been so intoxicated by the fumes of a neighbouring shoemaker in Totnes that she was 'reduced to writing thrillers'. Local environmental health department did a reading on the site to find it off the scale. The company disputes the damage caused but their insurers chose to settle. Interesting assumption here that thrillers are in some ways easier to write than more literary works. Far from true. In which case it might be worth saving your hard-earned cash and instead of spending it on a creative writing course (or MA) take a coach trip to Totnes and breathe in the fumes for a couple of days.

And, to confirm my doctor theory from above, I'm now facing a young posh rugger bloke in a taut Abercrombie & Fitch T-shirt with an impossibly rugged jaw who is on his mobile phone and discussing his 'two cases at the County tonight' where he's heading: 'Where's the stone? . . . Right. Fine . . . ya . . . yes, this guy is quite interesting I'll tell you about him when I'm not on the train . . . the other thing is this lady, how old is she? What's her BMI? . . . Roughly? And has she got DVT procolapsis [?], don't worry she needs to have some [trade name drug] before she comes to theatre . . .'

Good night to have a heart attack on the train.

28th January

A fever of writing *Nimrod* over the weekend and a major breakthrough. I can see where it's now all going to end. Both strands of the plot. Complicated to bring it off but it's promising and the thinking time invested in it has been worth it.

The *TLS* arrives carrying a review of a new collection of Graham Greene's letters and quotes something from one of his talks for the Third Programme: 'Isn't disloyalty as much the writer's virtue as loyalty is the soldier's?' Is it? Not in my book (note: another possible title), but an interesting glimpse into Greene's psyche.

30th January

Nimrod is pushing on. Another couple of months I think.

Tail end of last week a piece in *Publishing News* on publisher Cape in the light of them having published Anne Enright (Booker) and 'Stand-up comic and author', A. L. Kennedy (Costa prize). Dan Franklin from Cape points out that both have been published since the early nineties and this reflects Cape's long-term investment in writers they believe in – cue collective gnashing of teeth from the writers of the last decade they've canned who they clearly didn't believe in. Still, I bear no ill will towards either novelist. Good to see proper writing being rewarded for a change. Kennedy said that had she not won the prize she would have been looking for a miserable advance for her next novel; a major difference to her life determined by the outcome of a long judges' lunch. Vintage have rushed out the paperback of *Day* and expect to sell over seventy-five thousand. The difference a prize makes to a career is staggering. I remember Mark Haddon saying when he'd won some prize for *Curious Incident* that he was now invited to sit at the literary top table. He was no different a writer beforehand, just didn't have the statue and cheque to prove it. Goes without saying there are hundreds who don't.

Granta rejected the short story I mentioned to the editor at the Xmas party. The literary editor 'didn't fall in love with it'.

Incidentally, apropos *Nimrod*, I've now emailed a man who has a very useful website on capital punishment. He seems to be the fount of all knowledge on hangmen, the judicial process etc., so I've sent him a couple of questions I need to address before I press on with the story. I can't find out how long it would take between the verdict and a hanging. Crucial for the plot. Also very sparse information on the condemned cells in Pentonville.

Got back from the post-box to find a stern letter from the Office for National Statistics on the mat. It's a 'monthly inquiry into the production industries' form and I'm obliged by law to complete it for my 'business'. If I don't I might get fined. There is, of course, no payment for completing it and walking it round to the post-box. The tone of it is aggressive. It covers my period of business for January this year. I've filled it in. So – income (in thousands) NIL (thousand). Employees – NIL (I don't count myself I don't think, although maybe I should). There's a space at the bottom for explaining 'trade fluctuations' from last year so I explain that I'm a writer on the verge of extinction, as I was last January, but now more so, and would welcome any EU handouts that might be available – or possibly some thermal underwear. I hope they have a sense of humour but suspect not.

7th February

Taking a brief break from working at home to visit the accountant this morning to see if I can claim against tax the two years I spent on failed projects.

News through that a Channel 4 development person liked *Ivan* and *Whales* enough to want me to go in and see them (producer/head-cold-type meeting I suspect). She liked *Ivan* but found the comedy a 'bit broad'. She also read *Whales*, and that convinced her I could 'do character and tension'. Apparently they're looking for something in the *Teachers/Shameless* line. *The Store* might do but it might be a bit too 'high-concept'. Been tinkering with it quite a bit over the past couple of weeks to the detriment of *Nimrod* and I do think it has legs. The notion of a super-store which controls and runs society is quite interesting – by controlling the supply chain essentially they do. Done about two thirds of an episode, but it's taking me away from *Nimrod* which is now eighty thousand words in and is coming to a decent conclusion.

Email from the chair of the Bath Festival event to say she'd like a chat before the session so I will call her.

Email back from the history of hanging website man kindly answering all of the questions I asked him, including the one about the condemned cell. Apparently it was bigger to accommodate the three shifts of warders who kept suicide watch on the prisoner. The lights in the cell were never extinguished, but he was allowed a beer ration, newspapers and an improved diet. Duration between sentence and hanging, approximately three weeks: i.e., the week following three clear Sundays after the verdict has been passed. This is assuming he's not insane. If there was any doubt about his sanity the Criminal Lunatics Act of 1884 allowed for his examination by a panel of three prison psychiatrists, and if he was found to be insane he would be reprieved.

Must spend the next few days on *Nimrod*.

8th February

Too much talk on the train for *Nimrod* so a quick one on the meeting with accountant 'Mike' yesterday. Not much joy on claiming time spent on failed projects against tax, but he thinks we're not claiming enough in expenses. Mike looks a bit like Keith Floyd and has a similar unsettling way of looking at you directly, as if every question he poses has been a tricky one and demands a more considered response than the one you've offered. His office was the most impersonal I've ever been in. Very large, quite cold, with cheap mock-mahogany office furniture, two sofas (leather), and no photographs or any personal touches whatsoever, just a couple of lousy mass-produced prints of Venice. Mike seemed curious about the writing business and asked how it was done. I tried to tell him. He said it must be lonely, all that time spent on your own. He'd seen a TV programme about J. K. Rowling who was in tears when she revisited the flat and café in which she wrote the first *Harry Potter*. But writing is not lonely. How can it be if the characters are real? I tried to explain that to him but I don't think he really understood. Anyway, I was eager to get away, unsure whether I was being charged for the conversation. He seemed keen to chat. He asked how much the company had earned this year. I told him it was about two-and-a-half grand. Of course you can't judge it all on the financial returns but in such a fragile world it has to be one of the markers.

Nimrod yesterday made a move in a strange direction. The two characters in the contemporary storyline did something I hadn't planned. Reviewing it today, what happened between them was inevitable and I'm glad it did, but it was one of those strange moments where the conscious part of your brain has to roll over and let the unconscious take over for a while. I wrote a whole novel allowing the unconscious part of my mind to dictate the plot (*A Town by the Sea* – 'Subtle to a fault' the *Guardian*). It cost me my publisher I think. People either loved it or hated it but it had to be written. Will this work still exist when I'm dead? Will I still be in print in ten, or even five, years' time? Unlikely. Does it matter? I think it does. To me, at least – not to anybody else. The solipsism of writers.

13th February

5.10 a.m. On the early train to work as always on a Wednesday. *Midweek* goes out live on Radio 4 immediately after the 9 a.m. news and the guests start to show up around 7.30 for undrinkable coffee and flaky pastries, assuming the taxis we've booked have arrived to collect them – which often they haven't, prompting panic and hysteria for half an hour. The pre-programme hour in the green room is vital to relax them in each other's company. Libby sails through the regular crises of late-arriving guests. She's seen it all and, having presented *Today* (the first female presenter to do so), can deal with anything. She's used to the studio door opening just as the red light goes on and a flustered guest being ushered to the seat facing hers.

The local book group last night discussed *Minding* and invited me along to blather on about it. Conversation on many elements of the book, the most interesting one with an English A-level teacher who asked about the psychological markers you put down when you write: how conscious are they? She wanted to know because her students are assessed on how they pick up and spot these markers in the texts they're studying. For me they're not conscious, not in novels anyway. Characters develop organically and you just have to trust they have a psychological integrity. She seemed pleased about this but said it didn't accord with how her students were marked.

What pleased me the most was that the characters in the book were discussed as real people and all of the women seemed to have genuine feelings for them, particularly Billy, the son. Jane, the disturbed central character, they felt for and empathised with. Somebody asked why I wrote in short scenes and I said that because I write on the train the scenes tended to be a journey-length long. They thought I was joking, but I look back at the early books and can spot the longer journeys (points failure at Redhill) by the length of the passages. We discussed the relationship between editors and writers and I explained that my agent has always been the first line of editing, and the most important one for me. She tends to go to the heart of the problems with a novel before it gets sent out (or not if these problems are insoluble). This is rare nowadays. I was asked what she had changed or suggested about *Minding* and I said she hadn't suggested much at all. Then I remembered that actually she had. The first draft saw Jane being shot dead in a ludicrously operatic climax. Deborah suggested this was 'worth looking at' – she's never more prescriptive than that. So I looked at it and rewrote the end and the novel is much better for it.

Following last night I've made a conscious decision to try and raise my profile. Only two of the book group had heard of me as a writer – and that was only because I know both of them socially and had probably at some point told them. This lack of profile is frustrating. Self-deprecation is a safe default position but it doesn't help. If you're not seen to be serious about your own work why should anybody else take it seriously? Second is to tart myself round a bit more. I've avoided this for fifteen years but have to change. So I've emailed the British Council website to ask why I don't appear on their list of 'most important UK and Commonwealth novelists (living)'. There are hundreds of them. No response so far so I wait to learn how important I am.

Nimrod is still progressing well. Now the 1912 storyline has veered off in an unexpected direction, but, as with the contemporary storyline, I'm happy to let it run for a while. A new character cropped up: one of the warders on death watch. His name is Jebb. Son of a farmer from the Isle of Wight who worked at Parkhurst and was sent over as one of the death-watch minders to Reilly. Jebb is a likeable, affable young man, set apart from the other warders. He walks the city at night without a map and seems to have no need for sleep. Reilly takes to him, encourages him to sketch. The part he plays is now central to the final section of the book; last week he didn't exist. He came about because of a conversation I had with John who has spent much of his life in prison but is now going straight and who I see every week or so. John has read most of my stuff and is a good critic, as well as being a good writer and, more important, a good friend. He told me about the lottery which took place among warders up and down the country when there was a call for death-watch duty. If you were selected you were sent to London to oversee the condemned man until he was hanged. I liked the idea of an idealistic young man coming up to the city for the first time under such circumstances and encountering Reilly, and so Jebb was born. John also told me about the time he spent in Strangeways in his twenties. One of the cells was very cold and had an appalling atmosphere. He later learned that this was, of course, the condemned cell.

The WGA strike has now been resolved in time for the Oscars. The American writers seem to have got what they wanted in terms of residuals. Time to send *Cockroach* off and earn some nice rejections from the other side of the Atlantic.

A couple of days ago I spoke to the woman chairing the Bath Literature Festival event. She suggested something that worked well last year was that each author read the other's novel and choose a bit to read out and talk about. Clever plan. Forces us to read the work which we would probably only have pretended to do. Patrick's paperback arrived through the post yesterday so I'll make a start, but it's hard to avoid it in the press because his publishers have taken out full-page ads (colour) for it in the Sundays. Must try the next novel on them. Change trains at Gatwick and pick up the 6.05 a.m. Gatwick Express. I intended to do a bit of work on *Nimrod* but too tired. Hope for a snooze but, at the last minute, a man with very strong aftershave gets on with a female work colleague he's clearly trying to shag. Both cheaply power-dressed and wearing eye-watering scents they sit down directly behind me in the otherwise empty carriage. He has a bad toe, he announces, the result of him kicking the shed door last weekend. 'Why?' she makes the mistake of asking. 'It's a long story,' he says, then regrettably tells it. Get to work at 6.45 a.m. and find email reply from the British Council following my plea to be allowed on their 'most important contemporary writers (living)' website. I read it twice eating my bacon and egg McMuffin but couldn't work out whether it was a slightly starchy brush-off or a polite statement of position. It was explained that they currently have more than 200 authors on their waiting list to be added to the site and keep a note of authors they consider should be added. The site 'includes authors we work with plus major prizewinners from the UK and Commonwealth'. The lucky ones are selected at a twice yearly editorial board meeting but because they can only add between five and ten authors a month, 'the waiting time can be considerable'. The email closes with the promise: 'I will add your name to the waiting list to be put to the board.'

Seems there are others clamouring for attention and as I'm not a major prizewinning novelist (no need to rub it in) or ever get invited to jollies abroad at the British Council's expense I don't qualify. Worse than that I don't seem to be in the list of two hundred – yes two hundred – authors currently being considered for inclusion by a powerful all-party editorial board who meet twice a year to deliberate. What a palaver! Why do they need to meet at all? I suppose they get a decent meal out of it. Anyway, if I was among the two hundred she would have mentioned it – so I'm not. I, therefore, fall into the desperates' category – those who have dared to ask to be included. This is useful in reminding me where I stand in the league table of importance of UK and Commonwealth writers (living) – it's at least at 201 – plus the number of authors already on the site (several hundred – say eight hundred) so I'm ranked (assuming I'm at the top of the list of stragglers which I'm probably not) about 1001th in importance. Don't these people understand I'm a literary stealth bomber? I might have a considerable wait before (and if) I'm ever included. I'm fifty-two years old this year. I hope the wait is not too long. I write a rude reply, then delete it and sent back an airy 'Thanks'.

20th February

Bath Literature Festival this coming weekend – so my literary festival debut. Patrick Gale's appearance on *Richard & Judy* is on the festival website's front page so he should get a decent audience who will have to put up with me too. Perhaps I won't have to say anything – just sit there dribbling or picking my nose. Nearly finished his book. Not usually my kind of book – but I quite like it. Not that it isn't elegantly written – it is. Just that like a lot of the contemporary fiction I read nowadays it feels like it's written from the outside in. Doesn't mean you don't engage with them. Just that you don't feel for them. I don't, anyway, but clearly thousands do because the book is currently at number eleven in the Amazon sales rankings (*Minding* is at 473,000). See from his website all of his forthcoming appearances – Far East tour, Arvon foundation courses, playing his cello somewhere. The life of a recently promoted Premiership novelist. Feel no resentment towards him but slightly irked by the thanks at the back of his new book to the foundation that paid for his stay in some European capital where he finished writing his book. Maybe I'll see if they'll stump up something towards a first-class season ticket so I can at least continue writing *Nimrod* without having to put up with the inane babble of mobile phone conversations around me or people talking about the cause of their fractured toe.

Spent a good weekend in Florence with Julie and on the plane on the way back the woman next to me asked what I thought about the Patrick Gale, seeing me reading it and having seen it being discussed on *Richard & Judy*. 'I didn't fancy it from the way they were talking about it,' she said. I felt a bit disloyal to Mr Gale who I've never met but felt I had to be honest. Julie whispered that I should tell her to read my book instead – to which I whispered that there was no way I was going to tell her to read my book – or, indeed reveal that I wrote books. 'Well go to the toilet and I'll tell her,' she offered.

I declined. Julie has never been shy of promoting my works, whereas I adopt the opposite approach.

Wandered around the Uffizi while we were there, feeling astonishingly ignorant of what I should be appreciating, just enjoying the art and the atmosphere like a good meal for the mind. An American father was lecturing his two young daughters (in front of some epic and famous painting) about the Renaissance. It was fascinating. The kids were fascinated too and it was good to see. Made me feel better about the world. By contrast, using the Gents on the way out, I overheard two young American male students, presumably having spent two or three hours contemplating some of the greatest artistic masterpieces of the last six hundred years. They were discussing whether it was possible to 'shit out of your mouth'. The consensus seemed to be that it was.

Email from Fay to say that yes, we can now send *Cockroach* to the States. And that's about it. *Nimrod* now nearly ninety thousand words. One big push and it'll be all over and I can have my mind back again for a while.

Incidentally, now found useful new displacement activity. Bought a blood pressure monitor because the nurse who gave me my flu jab in the winter said my BP was high and I should keep an eye on it – 190 over something – which, looking at the graph on my Omron Digital Automatic Blood Pressure monitor (MX 2 Basic) is very high. Just taken it and it's now 142 over 92 which is only mild hypertension, so things are looking good and five minutes have been wasted so it's back to *Nimrod* which, for some reason, I find myself wanting to delay finishing. Completing a novel is, of course, the best bit; the time between writing the title on the first page (superstition dictates I always do this after completing it, though I tend to find an epigraph during writing so that tends to be page 1 for the duration – in the case of *Nimrod* it's something from Leonardo da Vinci's notebooks about shadow) and getting the response from agent, family, friends and anybody who's unwittingly agreed to read the first draft. I never used to bother showing early drafts to anyone beyond agent Deborah and Julie, but now circulate them a bit more widely as other views are also useful.

23rd February

Arrived in Bath for the festival and have checked in to the hotel which, like many British hotels, is a pit: stiflingly hot, the carpets on the stairs filthy, a packet of crisps trodden in on one of the treads, an uneaten tomato-sauce-dipped French fry on the carpet on the landing, the place not decorated since the mid-sixties. The fan in the bedroom has been dismantled and the protective mesh lies face down on a table accompanied by a couple of rusty screws. The sink is nearly blocked. The window is half open, presumably because there is a slightly foul smell in the room. Two pleasant but distracted young girls person the desk. Something of a contrast to the décor, service and air-conditioning of the Florence hotel where we stayed last weekend which cost approximately half the price – the immaculate desk there staffed by three multilingual, cultured (if slightly disdainful), uniformed concierges.

I wander around Bath feeling that sense of dislocation you get from visiting a new place on your own. This in part was what my novel *A Town by the Sea* was about. Detour into Waterstones which has a prominent display featuring many of the books written by the festival's writers. Goes without saying that mine doesn't take up any of the valuable table space, but I do find two copies of *Minding* on the back shelves which is something. A young American girl calls across to her friend – 'Yes, HAMLET . . . by William Shakespeare.' Bath is appealing, but for some reason the things that remain in my mind of the hour spent wandering around looking for an off-licence are two overweight sales louts in shirts and ties outside a phone shop – both canted forward at a forty-five-degree angle eating cheese pastries, the pastry flaking off and drifting down like snow – and two sofas of T-shirted students in the middle of a precinct raising money for Rag Week by holding a twenty-four-hour conversation. One is on his mobile. The only shard of the conversation I catch is 'No, I'm not masturbating.'

Back in the hotel room I find my ligged festival ticket for tonight to see critic John Sutherland in conversation with John Mullan and Peggy Reynolds, who I know a bit as I've worked with her a couple of times on the radio. A good spirit. This might give me a steer for tomorrow. Parking in Bath, incidentally, is a nightmare. Have left the car about half a mile away but will move it a bit closer after six. The publishers have agreed to pay petrol and parking. There's a £100 appearance fee for tomorrow so when that arrives the total writing income for the current financial year will stand at minus £248 because last year's accountant's bill arrived last week for £348.

Didn't bring the Omron Digital Automatic Blood Pressure monitor (MX 2 Basic) with me but suspect BP will be high due to the sense of foreboding about tomorrow.

Oh yes, email from Fay last night reporting another nice rejection from a British TV company who read *Minding*, loved it, but felt it was too bleak for ITV. I reminded her that the last thing they produced ended up with the three main protagonists sprawled round a country house covered in their own vomit having all been poisoned. Another email from another company she sent *Ivan* to – the woman liked the writing but said I wasn't quite right for the script rewrite Fay had put me up for but was keen to see more and, of course, to be 'kept in the loop' of what I might be doing in the future. No joy from the young producers unfettered by the film industry. The director of the group loved *Ivan*, but the producer couldn't understand why Ivan had taken the corpse from the hospital back for his girlfriend to see – and if you don't understand that then *Ivan* is not for you so that's that.

The cathedral bells chime five. I do hope they don't chime every bloody hour through the night. Must shift the car, find something cheap to eat (not sure if publisher is picking up meals) and then go to the Guildhall to see Messrs Sutherland and Mullan.

Back now and in digestive chaos due to a combination of four cans of Becks Vier and the KFC I had in a joyless glass-fronted building close to the hotel. Didn't spot any other members of the British literary elite in KFC – Margaret Drabble or Tariq Ali, for example. Presumably they use Burger King. Glimpsed myself on the KFC CCTV when I was queuing. I don't recognise myself any more. Some old fat bloke has taken over my body. And why is he wearing that ludicrous leather jacket? Who is he pretending to be?

Sutherland and Mullan were, as expected, fluent. Peggy prodded them a couple of times but they would have talked for four or five hours, or possibly days, without interruption had it been required. The average age of the audience seemed to be late sixties/early seventies. A bemused elderly woman called over a male usher (identified by a red beauty-queen-type sash saying 'USHER' on it) to protest that somebody was sitting in her seat, only to discover that the ticket she had was for an event which had taken place that afternoon. She did, however, find her ticket for the Sutherland session and was guided towards the rear of the auditorium by the usher in the sash. The man sitting next to me asked the panel a question about ebooks and pulled out a black iPod-looking thing from his pocket – waved it around a bit and announced that it held four thousand books. Much harrumphing from the audience and the panel.

Slightly disconcerted to hear Mullan admitting he sometimes waited for others' opinions before confirming what he thought about a novel. I've always suspected this of the British lit. establishment. They hunt in packs. This is why once you're admitted to the inner circle you're pretty much fireproof. In fact much of what Mullan and Sutherland had to say about how novels were constructed I found myself disagreeing with. They are, of course, authorities and I am not so I must be wrong. Just as I was wrong when I took my English A-level and failed dismally (uncategorised). The problem was I just couldn't see what it was I was expected to see in the novels, plays and poems I was reading. I was convinced I was right and they were wrong. In the long run it worked out in that I think if I'd studied English at university I might never have become a novelist and the world would have been cruelly denied my *oeuvre*. Also, though, it might go some way to explaining why my novels don't sell. I just don't fit. Clearly don't want to consider the other possibility – that they're all rubbish. Sutherland's book is called *How to Read a Novel* by the way.

The first time I wrote anything approaching a novel was at the desk in my parents' bedroom to which I retreated to do my homework after the daily misery of school. I was fourteen. My brain suddenly switched itself on just before my O-levels but until then I was hopelessly out of depth at a grammar school. I'd fluked my 11+ (I must have scraped it) but would have been more suited to and much happier at the local comprehensive. In the summer, as I sat at the desk and struggled with maths or physics or chemistry, the late afternoon sun was always at my back. One day, as a diversion from the homework, and taking a cue from the heat on my shoulders, I very quickly wrote the first few pages of a novel. *The Pier Song* was its title and it was the story of a tramp who lived on the beach in Brighton (street sleepers hadn't yet earned that appellation).

My attempts to follow this up were, however, discouraged at school. The establishment was an inflexible regime, run by a brutal cadre of senior management. The headmaster was tall and terrifying as he stalked the quad in his long, sweeping, black academic gown, and given to regularly handing out corporal punishment and verbal admonishments. His deputy head, 'Froggy', a short man, also gowned, was sinister and sadistic. Today he'd undoubtedly have been imprisoned for what he inflicted on his pupils: casually sliding a hand into a boy's shirt and painfully tweaking a nipple, routinely whacking pupils on the crown of the head with a hard-backed French grammar book, hurling board rubbers across the room with great accuracy and, worse, verbally belittling the less gifted of his charges and regularly handing out hour-long detentions. My English teacher was another of the head's deputies, and it was to her I showed an eight-page story I'd written after *The Pier Song* had filled me with enthusiasm. The new story was a spoof of, or an homage, I suppose, to *Tess of the d'Urbervilles*, which we were then studying. I wrote it, like *The Pier Song*, quickly and thought it had some merit. She didn't. I was called to her desk to stand and explain why I'd done it, almost as if I'd broken a window. I could find no reason that would satisfy her. All I could do was apologise and assure her it wouldn't happen again.

I arrived at the grammar school in Derbyshire as a shy, academically challenged eleven-year-old and emerged from it at eighteen, a blushing, anxious, insecure, late adolescent. Miraculously Sussex University allowed me a place and I spent my three years there hiding in the corner of seminar rooms so I didn't have to contribute, learning how to learn, and working on the radio station, which ultimately led to my career at the BBC.

On the way out of the Sutherland/Mullen session I overhear a woman emerging from another event saying, 'Well I suppose it's not important for authors to be able to talk well about their books in an interesting fashion.' Which gives me some hope for tomorrow – assuming the digestive chaos doesn't preclude me from attending. Don't want to make a name for myself as the first mid-list writer to soil himself live on the stage, like the guitarist of the Brit new wave band who apparently had bad stage fright, and Gary Lineker at the World Cup in Italy in 1990. In fact there's probably a non-fiction book or BBC Three series to be done on people who have soiled themselves in public arenas presented by the man with the very white teeth.

All of which . . . all of which has wasted an hour which could more usefully have been spent getting on with *Nimrod* which is what I had intended to do. And to which, if there's nothing on the telly, I will now return. Or I might pop out for a small scotch to settle the stomach. Incidentally, the cathedral bells chime the quarter hour, not the hour, so virtually no chance at all of sleep tonight.

24th February

Morning in Bath. Managed an hour on *Nimrod* last night, then watched *The Bourne Identity* on TV – by far the best of the trilogy. Hated the last one – just an extended fistfight extending across the roofs of several capital cities. Moronic cool, which is what Hollywood likes these days.

The cathedral bells did not chime all night but started up around six. Managed six hours of sleep then tried to have a shower – but the water was cold and dribbled like mercury from the head. Meeting Patrick and the session chair at two. Just reread the bit of Patrick's book I'm going to read out but stumbled a bit. Haven't read out loud for ages. Will rehearse it again before I check out. The cathedral bells now in full voice – must be calling people to the 11 a.m. service.

Digestive chaos thankfully quelled so go for the poached eggs option at breakfast and the 'seasonal fruits prepared by our chefs' – the 'chefs' presumably being the young school-refusers I glimpse when the filthy, kick-scuffed door to the kitchen bangs open. Like a knife thrower one of them is throwing something – vertical slices of bread I think – at a girl who laughingly fends them off before kneeling down to collect them and put them onto the cluttered work surface for distribution to the dining room. The two waiters are audaciously camp. One calls across the room to the other asking him why he's put out the white paper napkins instead of the black ones. 'Have we got a wedding on or something?' he wants to know. Unimagined wedding luxury – white paper napkins. A notice in the restaurant window begging for new staff – 'restaurant and reception' – to start immediately, at £6 an hour.

Moved the car in the car park this morning. One of the rough sleepers on the lower-ground level was prayer-kneeling beside an Austin Montego washing her hands with water poured from a litre bottle of Coke. She could easily be Jane, the protagonist of *Minding*. The homeless are more visible in Bath than Brighton – or perhaps at home I'm not usually up in time to see them emerge. Walked along the river. Massive tangle of tree trunks and other debris caught in the weir beneath the huge and beautiful grey stone bridge, diverting the easy flow. See two men with bedrolls heading for the fence from the river gardens where, presumably, they spent the night. First the bedrolls are chucked over, then they clamber. Their gentle collie dog, wearing a red neckerchief, noses through the gap ahead of them before waiting patiently for them to lead him to their pitch for the day. Both had *Big Issue* sellers' tags round their necks.

Checking out now. In three hours it will all be over and I'll have to find something else to worry about. I will not, however, have to worry about where I will lay my head tonight.

25th February

All over and seemed to go well. Virtually full house. Enthusiastic. Understand the Stockholm syndrome a little better now. On the platform I asked Patrick about his Richard & Judy experience. He said when the shortlist comes out each writer is phoned to be asked why they should be chosen. Shrewdly, knowing Richard and Judy have a holiday home in his area, he explained what a difference it would make to the local economy – people coming down to look for the locations. Enthusiastic applause from the full house.

Sold ten books after the event – ten! – doubled my sales in one fell swoop. Seeing the punters line up in front of Patrick thought I was in for a repeat of a signing I did about ten years ago alongside Roddy Doyle in Amsterdam. His queue stretched out of the bookshop, round the corner and out of sight, mine consisted of nobody – not a soul, not even somebody standing there by mistake. Roddy was sympathetic but didn't offer to buy one of my books. Nice bloke. The hotel we stayed at also housed some of the others who were also there to appear at the Crossing Border Festival in The Hague. The bar at 3 a.m. was like *Jools Holland's Hootenanny* on TV when he used to have decent guests. It was, indeed, Jools, who was playing the piano. Lou Reed was there looking ridiculously cool, unsmiling and unspeaking, plus twenty or thirty recognisable faces from the worlds of books and music. After it was over we got a lift back to the airport in a minibus with an American grunge band. A good couple of days.

Get home from Bath to find have left pyjamas at hotel. Call them up to be told that I have to give them a credit card number for postage if they find them, plus £5 'handling charge'. They were virtually clean so £5 seems a bit steep.

BP 148 over 97 (mild hypertension).

28th February

Following the excitement of the weekend emailed Tasja to ask if there was any chance of bringing *Minding* out as a proper paperback. Original publication was as a trade paperback. This would, I argued, give it a new lease of life. I still feel there is something left in it. Tasja responded by saying she'd had good feedback on the festival but on the tricky other issue they still had two thousand copies of *Minding* in the warehouse so chances of a paperback weren't good. We'd just have to rely on 'word of mouth' to get it out there. Failing that, they'll make a decent bonfire.

Email from a friend who works at the BBC but who also writes. Haven't heard from him for ages. Since we last spoke he's had twin daughters. He tells me each night he reads to them he remembers a scene in my BBC novel (*The Silent Sentry*) in which the son of the protagonist dreams of rabbits. This is quite a reassuring thing to know. He tells me he's still with the same agent but has just lost his publisher as he's now become an agent himself. Attrition rate of publishers about one a week at the moment.

Still no sign of pyjamas. Now emailed the hotel chain to ask where they might be and to protest at the £5 handling fee. As yet, no response.

BP 196 over 109. Grief. Appallingly high. Severe hypertension. Will check later.

Quick coffee with mate John to discuss certain aspects of *Nimrod*. Need some advice on Pentonville from him. I ask if he served time in there. 'Of course,' he says, as if it was a stupid question. We discussed the escape scenario of Reilly and he didn't buy it, nor did he buy the psychological profile of Jebb – all too neat. Says he's seen too many films in which an idealistic man helps out a wrongly convicted innocent. Would be more interesting if Jebb was darker, his motives more skewed. He's right. I'll look at it. We discuss the escape and decide on something that will seem more plausible.

Get home to find another letter from Office for National Statistics asking me this time for my business turnover for February and repeating the threat of imprisonment if

I don't fill it in promptly. As with January I tell them I have NIL employees, NIL turnover (thousands) and NIL exports (thousands). I don't mention the PLR payment because that's less than £200, nor the £100 from Bath (from which, in my accounts, I will deduct the £5 pyjama-handling charge, should they ever arrive). I hope I'm not the only member of the production industries to be contributing to this survey. If I am, expect dire newspaper headlines over next few months about the economy. Come to think of it the headlines are pretty dire so perhaps they're basing them solely on the turnover of 'Draxa Enterprises Ltd'. Recheck BP (it's now 12.04 p.m.): 145 over 94 so back to only mild hypertension.

29th February

Lunch today with friend Duncan at The Academy Club. Terrific place over a small restaurant in Soho. The building is old, the wooden floors slope to the left. The 'club' is a chilly uncarpeted bar which serves good red wine, resident dog asleep in a cardboard box under the laden bookshelf. When you've ordered food, a buzzer eventually goes and the barperson trudges down three flights and fetches it up from the restaurant. You can encounter anybody there – literary megastar, newspaper magnate, politician – or any one of a number of tweedy writers up for the day from the country. It's next door to the *Literary Review* office and Auberon Waugh usually turns up at two-ish, goes behind the bar and brings out five or six half-drunk bottles of red wine, which he cradles and then plonks at one of the long tables, joining or being joined by some of his chums, presumably to talk and drink the remains of the day away. Julie joined me up a few years back as a Christmas present and, since then, they've forgotten to ask me for my subs. Does make it slightly anxiety-provoking when you arrive and press the ground-floor buzzer to announce yourself. They've always let me in but soon I suspect they'll demand I settle my bill before I can come up the stairs. On the half landing on the way up you can look out across a small courtyard into the eccentric office of a British film company in which two or three young people are always working. I think it's Merchant Ivory because their mail is in a folder behind the front door.

During coffee the conversation turns from literature and the parlous state of the BBC to thermos flasks. Even Duncan has succumbed. It's like the *Invasion of the Body Snatchers*. Duncan, incidentally, is the best-dressed man in the BBC. He can't stand bad coffee so he now brings it to work in a flask. I bemoan the fact that tea tastes awful in them and he says it's important to do two things: never drink out of the plastic cap – use a cardboard cup – and get a bottle brush to scrub out the inside. Good tips. I tell him about progress of *Nimrod*. I have now written the final chapter but the penultimate one (or two) remain unfinished. He asks to see it. I tell him I remember something he said about reading the first draft of *The Repentant Morning* (a Spanish Civil War set piece) – that the plots were resolved like trains coming into a station. Absolutely right, of course. Very conscious about this as *Nimrod* comes to a halt. There are six or seven plots that could be resolved in this way, still wondering how to do it but not too neatly. Think I've found a solution to the end, and now I think I've found a way of concluding Reilly's appearance.

'Do you remember those tartan thermos flasks from your childhood?' he asks. I tell him I do. I also remember tartan rugs spread on the beach at Sutton on Sea, and sand in the bed at 'Breakwater Bungalows' where, as a family, we used to go every year, and the agony of sunburn on my knees. I remember, with my brother and sister, being taken by my dad every morning along the prom. to buy a comic from the newsagent's – usually a 'Summer Special' edition. Reading would never be as good as it was then. Spoke to my mum on the phone yesterday and she tells me Dad's in pain. His legs are giving him gyp and the pain seems to have spread all around his body. It makes him cross. My dad taught me to read as a child. I was hopeless at school but, tenderly, he coaxed me into understanding. He was the popular headmaster of a small village infant/junior school. My mum was an avid reader and would pass on her thick, well-used, American paperbacks to me: Don Passos, Ayn Rand, James Michener, Evan Hunter, Marilyn French, Raymond Chandler, John Steinbeck. She didn't fetishise books like I do. They were carriers for the message, that's all. Once read they were passed on or sold back to the secondhand shop. I grew up with a yearning for a strong narrative and it took me years to begin to appreciate the slow burn of English fiction. But give me a good American novel over an English one any day.

Phone message from the Bath hotel. Regretfully they have not found the pyjamas. Meeting at Channel 4 on Monday.

3rd March

Pick up *TLS* and read the lead review of the collected letters of Joseph Conrad. Didn't realise how awful the end of his life had been. Gout-ridden, poor, suffering from recurring bouts of malaria during which he'd wake up and speak in his native Polish. He would have fitted in well at my agent's Christmas party. It wasn't until the publication of *Chance* late in his life that his reputation was established and his books began to sell. His agent, a man called Pinker who also had Henry James and H. G. Wells, used to send him a cheque each week and effectively ran the family's affairs. Conrad owed him over £2000 but they fell out.

Meeting at Channel 4 on way into work. Brisk, friendly, a repetition of what Fay had already told me – that they were looking for something in the *Teachers/Shameless* line. Development person said she'd look at anything I sent in so I'd better get on with something.

Get into work to find a message from publisher to call her. Good news, she says, tantalisingly. I call. I've been shortlisted for the Mind Book of the Year. The only novel on the list. Lord Melvyn gives out the prize. I've read a couple on the list and my chances are slim but being shortlisted is significant and for once the judges have proper credentials (Fay Weldon, Blake Morrison and Michèle Roberts – no sign of Howard from the Halifax advert or any footballer's wife, soap star, Richard, Judy, Tony Parsons or Christopher Biggins). Must email the British Council to see how it affects my standing. There's a reading event at Foyle's and a dinner in May. Strictly embargoed so Tasja says I mustn't tell anybody until it's officially announced in mid-March. Spend rest of morning emailing and phoning around to tell people and telling them not to tell anybody else. Julie emails back to say she's v. pleased and was on the phone to a friend of ours when she got the news, who she also told but made him swear he wouldn't tell anybody else.

At coffee machine filling the thermos flask for journey home when I pause to talk to colleague, Chris. He says he has about five or six flasks at home of varying sizes. People always buy him one at Christmas. I tell him about my disappointment at the quality of the tea stored in them. The only one he uses regularly, he says, is a plastic-lined one which doesn't taint the tea at all. Might therefore have to buy a second flask for tea only and keep the current one for coffee.

10th March

Finally finished *Nimrod* at the weekend. Not much to say, but want to note the date I completed it. Will sit on it (not literally) for a few days or weeks before I send it off to Deborah. Not quite sure about the end. Think it works but will come back to it. Feels like I've been writing it forever, but looking back I see it was begun in October, so only six months which makes it the quickest I've ever finished. Just feel spent now, all the words used up.

14th March

Still feel no urgency in sending *Nimrod* out. This is unusual for me. Usually crave the validation a new book brings with it. Doesn't seem so acute at present. Think the shortlisting has something to do with it. It's sufficient to throw the monkey off my back for a while. There's still something not quite right about *Nimrod* at present. Can't quite work out what it is. I think Reilly steps away from the narrative too much about halfway through and although all the other storylines are focused on his death sentence they feel a bit mechanistic. Don't know. Lost that all-too-important distance from it. Be interesting to see what responses it gets from the two or three people I've asked to read it.

A piece I contributed to an event at the Brighton Fringe a couple of years back is being used in a book called *The Brighton Moment*. The princely fee of £25 is due. Round Robin email from the editor of the book (a local author) to thank all the writers for their contributions and apologise to those not chosen for the live festival event to celebrate the publication. I wasn't one of the lucky few to be chosen. However, she invites those not reading to come along anyway (presumably paying to get in). Therefore decide to check the names of those reading against the British Council list of major UK and Commonwealth novelists (living) to see how many of them feature in it. None.

There's something deeply cringe-making about being labelled a local novelist. It reeks of being second rate. Of course, when you're dead that all changes. But while you're alive it's a badge you should never wear.

26th March

Wife and daughter Sarah have read *Nimrod*, both under-standing, as always, that all I really want to hear are positive noises. But loyally both think it works and, most importantly, care about the characters. Been reluctant to send it off but have just done so, by email, and had an email back from Deborah to tell me it has arrived safely. Deborah's eyes are bad so she's going in for a cataract operation and will read it when she's regained her sight. We agree to meet for lunch to discuss it in a month's time, after the London Book Fair, of which we are again on the cusp, therefore literary London is in a frenzy of inactivity getting ready for it. I ask Deborah if we can have another crack at foreign publishers with *Minding*, but no response to the suggestion.

Had intended to spend today writing a review for the *Literary Review* which I foolishly agreed to do. What I really want to do for a while is absolutely nothing. Instead I have to manufacture an opinion on the new Sebastian Barry novel. About halfway through now and it seems good enough. Problem with reading books for review is that you don't read them as you would for pleasure. You're forever circling words, underlining passages, so that when you go back through you'll have sufficient bits to quote to back up your thesis – whatever that might be. For the most part it's simple: it's OK. It works. But that's not enough really.

Had a nice note from Simon Gray, to whom the publishers sent *Minding*. Kind words from him. He says of the characters, 'You look after them very well, it seems to me, all of them.' The note has his address and email at the top of it but I'm not sure whether I should thank him. Probably not. Because he'd then have to thank me for thanking him and it could therefore go on forever. But notes like that mean a huge amount. Books, as friend Duncan once observed, are quiet things. They're not designed to be paraded in huge auditoriums under TV lights. They should be passed politely from hand to hand, like secrets. Good to see that Gray's new book is getting universally rave reviews and wide coverage.

Emailed *The Store* to Fay just before the Easter weekend. Chased her up and she apologises for not having got back to me. TV and chocolate intervened. She did, however, start it last night. She didn't finish it, but will this weekend and promises to get back to me on Monday. Clearly not in a fantastic hurry to find out what happens to the characters otherwise she wouldn't have been able to put it down. I suspect agents read manuscripts like writers read books for review – assessing their potential rather than simply immersing themselves in them.

8th April

Clawed the manuscript of *Nimrod* back from Deborah because it still needs work, which I have nearly finished so will get draft two off tomorrow or the next day. Still unsure about the end but it's getting there.

Spoken to Fay about *The Store*. She genuinely seems to like it. Says it feels younger than the last couple of pieces (*Ivan* and *Whales*). She says she thinks it would work on BBC Three so she has sent it off to a few people, including the Channel 4 development person I met and the producer I had dealings with over *Ivan*. The wait begins. She doesn't mention she's had any response on *Cockroach* so that's probably dead in the water now. Eight or nine screenplays now languishing unproduced in my files. Still feel I learn a little more each time I write one and another little bit of me dies when nobody picks it up. Unproduced scripts are like orphans.

I've now sent off the review of the Barry book to the *Literary Review*. I ended up liking the first 280 pages very much and hating the end. Tried to write a balanced review and not let my feelings over the end overshadow the rest. They promised to mention *Minding* and the Mind shortlist, of which there has not been a single mention in any newspaper, including the trade press. Might, therefore, not be the fillip to my career I'd hoped, but at least I'll get a decent lunch out of it.

Khaled Hosseini is coming in tomorrow for *Midweek*. His novel *Kite Runner* has now been sold in thirty-eight countries, and has been made into a critically acclaimed film. Can't begin to conceive what this must feel like to an author. Wonder if he'll behave grandly or be nice and humble like some of the most famous people are. It's the C-listers who tend to give the production staff the hardest time.

9th April

Khaled Hosseini was, of course, fluent, good-looking, interesting, intelligent and appropriately bemused by his massive global success. He's here for the Galaxy awards tonight with Richard and Judy – a star-studded event.

BP 144 over 93. Mild hypertension.

22nd April

A few things to catch up on. Meeting a couple of days ago with the BBC producer who wanted to make *Ivan*. She read *The Store*, liked it, and offered four pages of detailed notes. Without any commitment from them slightly loath to make any changes, so speak to agent Fay about it. She calls the producer to discuss how to proceed. L. says she wants to push it through the system but can't promise how long it will take for her boss to read it, and can't guarantee anything until he does. Fay says for her to go ahead and, meanwhile, if we get anything back from the others we've sent it to she'll let her know.

Lunch yesterday with agent Deborah for the all-important discussion on *Nimrod's Shadow*. Deborah doesn't do praise. After the preamble she says, 'We have a lot to talk about.' Heart sinks because obviously all I want is for her to say it's perfect, she'll send it out and it'll sell for vast sums around the world. Deborah's instincts are that there's something amiss with the character development in the contemporary plotline. We discuss the main characters and then veer into talk about Keith, a secondary character. 'Tell me about him,' Deborah says in the unsettling way she has. I parrot a few lines from the book, but I know that she wants to know his backstory, i.e., the stuff that's not in the book. I make something up. Deborah adds a few thoughts (dead parents, sister in Yorkshire married to a solicitor, kids and dogs; all sounds very feasible). After an hour or so of this gruelling stuff I come away and try and distil what it is she wants me to do. Deborah has a way of asking questions which make you ask questions of yourself. It's important to process these questions over a number of days then go back to the manuscript and try to apply them. I don't think we're talking a major rewrite, just a few tweaks. As I said, I'm not sure whether she likes the book. We had a similar conversation after the Spanish Civil War novel I wrote, *The Repentant Morning*, which I came away from feeling utterly deflated. She then went away and sold the tweaked book for a very respectable sum. 'Do you think Portobello will want it?' I ask her as we part. 'I hope so,' she says. Then, as an afterthought, 'I'd very much like to sell you in America.'

28th April

Still nothing back on *The Store* so spent yesterday tweaking it in accordance with L.'s notes. Still awaiting Deborah's notes on *Nimrod* and have done all I can on it. I know I can't do any more because each change I now make is visible and seems crass, so just making it worse.

The Sebastian Barry book is now out and I'm relieved to read three reviews which echo my own thoughts about the ending of the book. Shame really. It would have been much, much stronger without it. Makes me feel glad to have Deborah as an agent. I know she wouldn't have allowed an ending like that without me putting up a staunch defence.

2nd May

At Foyles last night for the Mind shortlist reading event. Spent some time talking to Blake Morrison who says he liked *Minding* and couldn't work out why he hadn't heard of me before. I said I wasn't surprised, I hadn't heard of me before. Evening supposed to be hosted by Fay Weldon but, by 6.30, she hasn't arrived so after the Mind man gets up and effects the introductions, Blake Morrison takes the stand to announce her absence – at which point somebody from Mind at the back of the room holds up a mobile phone and informs us that Fay's missed her train. Michèle Roberts (one of the three judges) stands in for her and manages to be fluent and engaging, speaking very impressively off the cuff as she introduces the readings. Huge clap of thunder then follows and an immediate heavy downpour – the air is charged by ions and the mood of the room lifts. We've been told to prepare about five minutes. Having worked in radio for the last twenty-seven years I know how many words constitute a five-minute reading – and have whittled down my extract to run at precisely that length. Not so the others. The longest reading goes on for over twenty minutes – and when the reader sits down he whispers to me, 'A bit long, I think.'

'I thought you were going to read out the whole book,' I whisper back. But then, seeing his deflated look, add that he read very well – which he did.

On the way out one of the organisers asks if I want to know whether I've won or not before the event in two weeks' time. This is standard practice with Mind – being a mental health charity they don't want to put people through too much emotional turmoil. I say that I do want to know, but already know I haven't – just something in the vibe of the room – although Michèle Roberts does give the game away a bit when she begins her introductions by questioning why the books have been presented in the order they have. 'They're not in alphabetical order,' she muses, 'and not in order of . . . ah, merit.' So bad luck for Darien Leader who kicks off the event.

Speaking to Tasja afterwards she says she was disappointed that *Minding* didn't get at least longlisted for the Booker. Apparently one of the judges liked it a lot and reported the fact to her agent, who then passed it on to Tasja. We discuss *Nimrod*. She asks when she can see it. I tell her it'll be with her when it's been released by Deborah – which I hope will be soon. I could, of course, pass it to her there and then or email it direct, but this would be contrary to the well-established and formal procedure for the submission of manuscripts.

Friend John found a body on the beach on Tuesday morning when he was walking the dogs. He reported it by email in typical John style. On Sunday, he says, he'd found a mobile phone, the next day a wallet, both of which he took to the police – then, on Tuesday, the body. Not having his phone with him he dashed to the prom. and flagged down a man in a lorry. Man didn't want to get involved and refused to call the police so John had to go to a public phone box, all the while worrying that the tide would carry the body back out to sea. It was an elderly man, he thought, but the sea had washed his clothes up to cover his face. John said it was like stumbling into a scene from *Nimrod's Shadow*, which he has nearly finished reading. He didn't seem unduly concerned about his experience. His life has been full of such dramas – delivered to Barnardo's shortly after birth, a brutal failed adoption, a life of crime culminating in armed robbery and fleeing from the Flying Squad across the Channel to join the French Foreign Legion from which he deserted, coming back and giving himself up to begin his first really long stint behind bars (which is where I first met him when I was in there making a Radio 4 documentary). We've been friends since. Kindred spirits somehow. Anyway, more details from him tomorrow I hope.

Email back from BBC producer L. who thanks me for the tweaked *Store* script. She thinks the changes I've made work – bar one – but it's not a major issue at this point. She'll 'shove it under the nose' of her boss when he comes back from leave after the bank holiday – she's cleared the decks of the other stuff so it'll be the only thing he has to read. Like the process of getting the manuscript from agent to publisher, getting a script read by people who have the clout to make it has a similar complex choreography dictated by power, practice and ego.

19th May

Displacement activity is much less important when not writing a novel. The last weeks have seen a number of developments but because I haven't been writing I haven't felt the need to break away to catch up with the journal. So, first thing is that the Mind dinner has come and gone. As predicted I didn't win but was gratified that the book I felt should have won actually did. A poignant and beautiful memoir by Martin Townsend on his father's bipolar disorder and the effect it had on the family (*The Father I Had*). Julie and I went up to London for the lunch which went on for three hours, hosted genially by Melvyn Bragg. Spent some time talking to Fay Weldon who says she was ashamed not to have made the readings evening. She said she had been looking forward to it. I told her about the thunder. She asked what I was there for. I told her I was on the shortlist. She said she must have recognised the fact that I was a writer from the other side of the room because she was drawn to come across and talk to me. She said she liked the novel. All in all a good day. Agent Deborah was there but had to dash off at three for a meeting at Faber. Tasja and head honcho of Portobello turned up. Julie and I arrived flustered after buying a pair of shorts for our son in the hellhole that is Abercrombie & Fitch. Deafening music. Dim lights. Library-tall shelving. Good-looking youngsters posted on every corner asking if they can help and wishing us well. An Adonis with a bare torso part of the welcoming party at the door. Very unsettling and certainly not a place for anybody over twenty-five years of age. It's also virtually impossible to find your way out. No exit signs, so you walk round in the fragrant semi-darkness, slightly panicked, thinking you might be stuck in there for the rest of your life.

All in all felt very well supported at the Mind lunch but somehow felt I'd let everybody down by not winning.

Deborah still has the second draft of *Nimrod's Shadow* which she said she will get to shortly and, if it works, get it off to Portobello. She talked to Tasja about it at the Mind lunch. Now it's out of the way I look through inert film and TV projects to see if anything could be reignited. Decide to email promising young film director to tell him I'm looking for a project and ask how he's fixed. Expect no reply as I sent him a copy of *Thought About You* last January and received no response. Astonished to get a reply within five minutes apologising that he hasn't been in touch and that he didn't respond to the script I sent. Even now it's printing out. He says he has had three projects which have come to nothing and asks if, despite his track record, I'd like to meet. I tell him I would and send off *An American Cockroach* so we have a couple of things to discuss. I tell him that I persist with him because I like his work (which I do) and wouldn't pursue many other British directors in such a way (huge arrogance on my behalf of course as there are no other British directors currently interested in my work – and an obvious lie). However, if we do embark on a project and it dies or goes cold he must promise to email and tell me, not just go silent like he did last time. He emails back to tell me he'll book a table at The Ivy and we'll meet on Monday if that suits.

So I think by the end of today there might be another film project on the go. Mid-list writers can afford no pride. Having rewritten *Cockroach* it's much tighter. The first draft, frankly, was all over the place. Emailed Fay to tell her about developments. She says to play it by ear and see what's on the table.

Nothing back yet on *The Store*, but feel a slight sense of optimism that there are a few possibilities out there again. Really should start casting around for another novel idea but there's no rush. If Portobello do want to publish *Nimrod* it won't happen for at least twelve months and I don't want to burden Deborah with another manuscript to hawk round. I ask myself the question, and not for the first time, why? Why the need to cast around for another novel to write? Why the compulsion? Is it some kind of addiction? Who cares? OK, I do, but why? Maybe one day I'll be able to answer that question.

Today's train conversation now crashes into my mental space (woman, late twenties, trendy): '. . . No, it's the Catholics. Oh, absolutely . . . yeah . . . yeah . . . no, it's not so much that he . . . he'll use it. He's clever, he'll use it as a device not to do anything until he . . . yeah. I mean use it more as a bargaining . . . he's utterly . . . yes, it's something that makes my palms sweat. I hope so because . . . yes. Well you can understand, he's like that.'

20th May

A noisy patrician man is on the phone even before we leave Brighton which doesn't bode well for the journey ahead: 'So if I start off the meeting by explaining the, the flow charts . . . So what did they actually? . . . Ah, I'm now beginning to see what's happened. In that case . . . I'm actually stuck on a train . . . You actually need to explain the process and put in a bit more, bit more detail. I gather he'd just got back from region . . . There was no regional representative there yesterday? . . . If Ray is there can you rehearse that? . . . OK I think that's recoverable. Yes, it's the, it's the . . . Yes.' Call ends.

Call two (two minutes later). '... Just to go back to the meeting yesterday. What was the aim of the meeting yesterday? Southwest? Yes ...' (and on and on).

Lunch meeting at The Ivy yesterday was affable. PYD had read *Thought About You* but there's not enough action in it for him and no surprises. He will read *Cockroach* before Thursday when he has a meeting to discuss his current projects with his agent, some bigwig who has access to development funds. He also wants to revisit *Whales*. I ask him about his career since his last film. The response was critically mixed which he said led to a couple of years of depression about the industry. Two big projects which were supposed to follow didn't come off. Either would have catapulted him into the major Hollywood league. Understandably he's wary about the next thing he engages with but the longer it goes on the more rides on it. I suggest he shouldn't listen to the critics. It's hard but you have to cut yourself off from them.

He tells me that one of the upsides of his previous flurry of fame is that he can always get a table at The Ivy. It's a great restaurant. My previous publisher used to take me there. I haven't been there for ten years and it's still the same. Waiters on casters. Attention to detail (as they'd say on *MasterChef*). Food on the menu you actually recognise. If you arrive early and alone they steer you to the table and immediately offer you a copy of the *Evening Standard* along with a drink so you don't look too tragic. I order water (I must be getting old). Menu the same. The same feel to the double-aspect room. It's the position of the place that makes it unique. It inhabits a V-shaped building with narrow streets on both sides. The windows are made up of diamonds of

94

coloured glass (blues and yellows and greens I think) which makes the atmosphere pretty magical and the light in the room special, like being inside a swimming pool, but the glass obscures the world outside so you could actually be anywhere your mind takes you, and at The Ivy it's always another place.

PYD arrives in cycling lycra, honed torso ridiculously evident. Fragrant and no sign whatsoever of sweat. I half stand and we shake. I go for the soup and haddock and chips. The soup arrives in a small metal-lidded dish which the waiter tips into the plate, shielding my clothes from splashes with the upturned lid. Very hot so takes about twenty minutes to eat. PYD is on a no-carb diet so has steamed spinach for his starter and steamed cod for the main. I feel unduly plebbish tucking in to my fish and chips. He has a personal trainer, he says. They meet at the park each morning at 6 a.m. Sometimes he pulls the trainer along on a sledge.

Anyway, we exchange phone numbers and I now await his response to *Cockroach*. Unlike *Whales* it's not an expensive or complicated film. You could do it for $2 or $3m with ease (I say blithely, knowing absolutely nothing about what films cost, but I'm learning how to bluff it like everybody else in the industry). He promises to let me know his thoughts before Thursday and sprints from the building.

When I get back to the office I email the producer to ask about the progress of *The Store*. Nothing back yet as obviously there hasn't been any but for a moment I imagine that I'm a player in the film industry. Then I remember I'm not and feel ashamed for wasting her time again.

27th May

Things are moving quickly on *An American Cockroach*. A couple of days after meeting PYD he emailed back to say bar a couple of reservations he liked *Cockroach* a lot and wanted to put it in the mix for his Friday meeting. He didn't think the script was quite ready to show yet but was happy to give his people a summary. Was I happy with that? I emailed back to say that I was, but on what basis were we proceeding? Get the usual response back to say that he wanted me to see his notes first, then write another draft on spec and if he was happy with that then there might be some money on the table. This, however, is contingent on his Friday meeting and his people liking it. If they do then his people will presumably talk to my people (Fay) and we can formalise something.

On Saturday the internet is down at home (as it is every other day) so have no access to emails. On Sunday daughter and boyfriend arrive for dinner and he patiently repairs the computer (again). When they've gone I check emails to find one from PYD to report that the Friday meeting was positive and the two people he met (his London agents – plural), were intrigued enough by his précis of the script to encourage him to pursue it. So he's doing some notes with a view to me rewriting it and getting a draft to them in two weeks. If they like it we can move to an option and development. All sounds positive but having been burned so many times before I email him back to say happy to proceed and will await a time for the meeting. Look back through this journal to see that *Cockroach* was finished in October 2007 so now eight months old and it has only now reached stage one. Many hurdles at which it can fall but at least it's in the race. Film projects need a natural momentum. They live fast or die slowly.

Nothing back on *The Store* bar a note to say the producer is still waiting for it to be read by her boss, but an initial conversation she had with him was positive. He liked the sound of the characters but warned that it couldn't be too dark as the BBC didn't want dark projects at the moment.

No news on *Nimrod*. Not sure if Deborah has read draft two and sent it out yet. Suspect not.

I realise that I'm now in a similar position to that of a year ago when I was awaiting response on *Whales* manuscript, *Whales* film and *Ivan* TV project, all of which failed. Perhaps the latest trio of projects has more hope, but it just points up the fact that you have to keep at it: keep doing it; keep pushing if you want to get stuff out there.

There's an old-fashioned toddler on the train this morning annoying the regulars and making writing impossible. Under two feet high, he looks like a mini-me version of Arthur Lowe (a bald circular head, very vocal, slightly pompous, speaking authoritatively in a language only he understands, dressed like a Second World War refugee). He has a large plaster covering his right eye and circular, wire-framed NHS glasses. He patrols up and down the carriage gesticulating, prodding people's arms and legs, looking into bags while his mother follows him a short distance behind, pacifying in his wake, making sure he doesn't fall into a table edge and damage his other eye. He seems a determined individual and she is remarkably patient with him. She has wisely not tried to trap him into a seat for the duration of the journey. After one further pass of the carriage she sits down and he settles on her knee. Now he's pointing out things through the window, explaining what he's seen, looking to her for reassurance and she's nodding in agreement, gently correcting the odd word and suggesting alternatives.

A train passes. 'Wheel!' Mini Arthur says, pointing.

'Train,' his mother corrects. 'Train.'

Mini Arthur processes this, nods and repeats: 'Wheel.' Mother kisses him on forehead. He jabs two fingers into his mouth and promptly drops off to sleep.

I miss my kids being that age. Falling asleep and waking an hour later with a blush on their cheek where they have nestled against you.

4th June

Yesterday I picked up the ringing work phone and heard: 'Soooooo . . .' It's agent Deborah with her characteristic greeting. She rarely identifies herself by name. We exchange a few quick pleasantries but I'm on tenterhooks. This is the verdict on *Nimrod*. 'I think you've done marvellously with the language,' she says. Huge relief. Her biggest gripe with draft one was the overly ornate Edwardian language so she now considers it sufficiently toned down. I wait but there seem to be no more outstanding issues to resolve. She's ready to send it off to the publisher. Huge relief, even more so when I remember the third or fourth call on the *Whales* novel last year, during which she announced she was going to ask a couple of other people at the agency to read it. This is Deborah's way of saying she doesn't like it and it needs a major rewrite or to be binned.

To celebrate, as I haven't heard from PYD for a week or so (bar a brief email during half-term pleading that half-term was getting in the way of work), I email him to ask about progress. We're approaching the end of week two since his meeting with his people, at which he promised to get them a draft within a fortnight. No chance of this now. I half expect nothing back but get a reply within the hour to say he is still reading and developing thoughts. 'I get more inspired with each read,' he tells me. He promises full notes within a couple of days and then we will meet.

So, three projects still alive – for now.

6th July

Things are moving on in a generally positive way following a meeting at PYD's home. I didn't really know what to expect when he invited me there for a lunchtime script session but he said he'd collect me from the tube station as it was a lengthy walk. He arrived in a small electric car and we set off along an avenue of very expensive West London real estate, finally coming to a halt at a pair of electric gates. The gates opened to reveal a huge and quite beautiful red-bricked Edwardian mansion (the only word for it, really). I assumed that PYD and his family inhabited a flat within the building but when we went through the front door into the massive hallway realised it was his – all his. The house was beyond elegant. The kitchen itself cost roughly half of what our house is worth. But the back was the biggest surprise. The rear wall had been taken down and replaced by glass so, having entered the portal at the start of the twentieth century, you exited into the future. On the house tour we encountered two builders fixing a leak in the roof and in the brief exchange between PYD and the men I learned more about him than I had done in all the time we had previously spent together. They deferred to him. He was lord of the manor. Perhaps this relationship was one of the keys to understanding why PYD lived in such a house and had such a life.

On the occasions we've had builders in we've furnished them with tea. Been polite, accommodating, accepted all of their lies about broken-down vans when they disappeared for two weeks on another job, tolerated their monopolising of the lavatory and the plaster footmarks across the bedroom carpet to the upstairs telephone where they'd been laying their bets. Yes, we'd got it wrong and PYD had got it right and this splendour was his reward. I liked him less but understood him more.

A couple of further meetings with PYD, a couple of tweaks to the script, a couple of lunches, and it went off to his people to pass judgement on whether it was a project they considered he should be pursuing. A positive response was delivered within a week so his people are now speaking to my person with a view to him optioning the script for twelve months. There's still work to be done on it (slightly concerned that he suggested his agents liked 'the skeleton idea' and thought 'there was lots of potential'), nevertheless at least the project is alive and is now over hurdle two. Fay is going for an option fee of £10,000 on the grounds of the work done and the past work done on *Whales*. She says she's unlikely to get it as PYD I think is optioning it himself – with his own hard-earned cash – so we'll probably get about £5 and a luncheon voucher. She's also going for 3½ percent of budget for the script. Again this is an initial bid but it means if the budget is $4m then I'll get about £80,000. PYD is away so it will be a while until the deal is sorted.

No news yet from Portobello on *Nimrod*. Now approaching six weeks. Emailed agent Deborah a couple of times with gentle enquiries over the initial response. I can't imagine they haven't read it yet which means they're either arguing over money, arguing between themselves as to whether they should publish it, or working out a kind way to say they hate it and they don't want to publish. Feel pretty sanguine about it, only because *Cockroach* is still alive. If *Nimrod's Shadow* was the only thing on the table I'd probably be tearing my hair out.

Email from BBC on *The Store* to explain the head man hasn't read it yet as he's concerned it's too dark. He wants outlines of the next five episodes to convince him it isn't too dark before he expends half an hour of his valuable time doing what I imagine he's paid to do – read scripts and pass judgement on them. I stew for a couple of days then email the producer back to suggest that perhaps the strength of the piece is in the characters and not the situation and perhaps we could meet to thrash out some thoughts on developing it a different way. She emails back to say she's going on leave but has been advised to take her phone with her and stay in contact as changes are afoot in her department. I already know from Fay that the top man has jumped ship – but I don't think many other people are in the loop, so perhaps this is the news she'll be given on her holiday. Either way, pointless doing anything with *The Store* for now.

So prospects remain fairly good at present. On past experience this could all change rapidly. Until contracts have been signed on both film and novel I won't celebrate, but still feel positive.

30th July

Nearly another month has passed and developments on all fronts. After waiting another few days for a response to

Nimrod's Shadow I emailed agent Deborah to suggest that surely the publishers had read it by now and was she therefore holding on to the bad news for some reason? Sheepish phone call the following day to explain that due to her technical incompetence the manuscript had not yet been delivered to them. What makes it more worrying is that they hadn't chased her up asking why she hadn't sent it. So it was finally delivered to the publishers (I feel I can still call them 'my publishers' until they turn the book down) the following day, seven weeks late. Deborah suggested we should expect a response within two weeks.

Three weeks passed. I called Deborah. She was away so I emailed the publishers to ask whether there had been a response. I wasn't asking Tasja what their verdict was, but just wanted to know if it was worth chasing Deborah before I went away on my holidays. Tasja responded with apologies to say she hadn't read it yet but promised a verdict by the end of August. I look back over this journal and discover that the final draft was agreed with agent Deborah on 4 June. I remain grateful that I do not have to rely on my writing to feed the family.

However, things are progressing on the film front. PYD has, indeed, now optioned the screenplay for eighteen months for £7500: £5000 to be handed over now, the rest split into two and paid up when two further rewrites have been done. He's hoping to get the money from the independent sector and intends, if all goes well, to shoot it next spring. Clearly there are a number of big 'ifs' between now and then; however, it seems to be at the top of his list of his priorities at present. The next two months are critical. My feeling is that if he doesn't get the budget by then he'll be off and working on something else. Anyway, draft three has been delivered to him and a response is awaited. We're off to the States on Saturday for a family holiday and it would be good to know that he was happy enough with the latest draft to send it out to the money people while we were away.

And, finally, the news of the BBC exec's departure has now been made public. He never did find time to read *The Store*, so it wouldn't have been worth writing the five outlines of other episodes. Channel 4 turned it down, but liked the writing and want to see anything else I might have. But there's enough out there at the moment waiting for the green light. If the film is made and the book is bought my stock will obviously rise – but things have a habit of not quite turning out how you'd hope so I'll try to rein in my optimism and will report back after two weeks away.

20th August

In San Francisco a week ago watching CNN on the hotel room TV when the news ticker across the bottom of the silent screen announces the death of 'British novelist and playwright, Simon Gray'. He would have been pleased to have made CNN. I feel profoundly touched by the death. Despite meeting him only once it feels like the loss of a friend. But I do feel as if I knew him, perhaps through his work, perhaps his journals. But very sad.

Now back at home and work to find little progress on the writing projects. Still awaiting the verdict on *Nimrod*, and have had an email back from PYD to tell me he's read the latest draft of *Cockroach* and feels it's moved on but he has lots of thoughts, suggestions and concerns. I don't like the 'concerns' bit. I reread it last night and there's something amiss with it. Having written a few drafts now it's becoming harder to look at it afresh. The logic that held the first couple of drafts together is now no longer there and I'm not convinced a new logic has been applied in its stead. This is what tends to happen when you're constantly rewriting using somebody else's notes.

The next draft I think will be critical and my feeling is that it needs to become something different otherwise it will simply be another police procedural with a twist at the end. Finance will be hard to raise. I'm beginning to understand what I should already have known: film is a director's medium not a writer's and every draft is designed to shift ownership from writer to director – your vision eventually becoming theirs to realise. Incidentally, Fay is still arguing over the contract so no money has arrived yet but she assures me it's only a matter of time. The issue seems to be the ceiling of what I should expect to be paid if the film gets made. My optimism has taken something of a dive over this but perhaps it's just post-holiday blues.

4th September

Because I'd been promised a verdict on *Nimrod* 'by the end of August', decided to pester agent Deborah to chase up the news. No response so far and can't be bothered to email for the third time so I email Tasja at the publishers to ask her direct. Get an 'out of office' by return explaining she'll be back by 'Tues 3nd Sept'. Tues is actually 2nd so assume 3nd is a mistype, unless it's Weds 3rd. However, later in the day an email comes through to tell me she's been away and is just back, has read the book and 'enjoyed it a lot', but was 'quite surprised by it'. Not quite sure what this means. Nobody else in the office has yet seen it but she wants to reassure me she'll be championing it. So the wait goes on but some relief that she liked it.

Still nothing back from PYD besides an email to tell me he was away with the kids. Therefore still no sign of the advance on the script, which I could do with as the credit card bill for America has just come in and I owe them £1100. Can't quite see how we managed to spend so much considering we also took quite a lot of cash, but it will have to be paid. In an attempt to pay it off I decide to have a flutter on the Booker Prize. I read one of the longlisted books on holiday and think it's worth chancing a tenner on so I enrol in the William Hill internet site and put some money down (the book stands at 10/1). Within five minutes the phone rings and the Barclays fraud squad are on the phone asking if I've just spent some money online on William Hill as my card has thrown up an alert. It seems they don't have me down as an inveterate gambler. I admit nervously that I have and manage to stop myself offering an apology. They then ask me if I also spent £20 in the local organic butchers that morning and £8.40 in Somerfield yesterday. I guiltily admit that I did and feel close to breaking and admitting all of my past mis-demeanours to them. Like a list of unsolved crimes they run through a few more payments, all of which I made (Sainsbury's, turps from B&Q, a restaurant bill). I sense the woman on the phone disapproves of almost all of the purchases and feel increasingly ashamed that I've been caught out spending my own money on frivolities like food and decorating items. She finishes by apologising for bothering me. I tell them I'm glad that my account is being so closely monitored given the lack of funds in it. Feel very unsettled by the Kafka-esque phone call. Still, the £10 bet remains on Steve Tolz for the Booker with the potential return of £100, thus cutting the credit card debt to a mere £1000 if he wins. We'll see if he makes the shortlist in five days.

5th September

Polishing off a new script on the train when today's interruption comes from a man who has just announced to the caller on his mobile that he's on his way to the British Library. 'The nose . . . the ear we know is Jenkins' . . . it was a short quasi-war with the Spanish, he tried to defend his ship and he lost his ear. It was pickled in a jar. Then we went to war with Spain. I think that's all I know . . . the War of the Potato is a good one, the Six-day War, the Six Years' War. . . Ya. Enjoy Perugia. Ya. Bye.'

Now back to the script.

8th September

Brief email back from Tasja at Portobello in return to me sending her a JPEG of one of Peter Messer's tempera paintings. I explain to her that it's the painting that features in the novel. She asks if, therefore, she should assume that Reilly is based on an actual person. I email back to say that he isn't but I visited Peter in his studio a couple of times to see how he worked; he helped me understand the process. Nothing back after that so I don't know if she's disappointed or relieved Reilly isn't real.

Email from PYD apologising that he hasn't been in touch – he was called in at short notice to do some filming in Ghana. However, he's back in a week and wants to put aside a day to go through the latest draft of *Cockroach*. I suggest a couple of dates and await confirmation.

Have now finished a new screenplay. It took an unexpected turn at the end which I'm pleased about as I think it makes it much more interesting. Couple of decent twists and turns, with a nice ambiguous ending. Inevitably the ambiguity will be lost should anybody decide to option and develop it. One more read through then I'll send it off to Fay for a verdict. For the first time I send off a script with some vague hope that somebody somewhere might actually want to develop it. Having a screenplay in active development with PYD gives you some kudos and allows Fay to trumpet it when she sends the script out. This means that, for the time being at least, my scripts will be read a bit more carefully just in case potential producers miss the next big thing.

Shortlist for the Booker announced and Tolz is on there so the bet on him is still alive. Also on the shortlist Sebastian Barry with the novel I reviewed for the *Literary Review*. Clearly the judges don't have the same issue with the end that I did.

Displacement activity today included doing a word count on this journal and I see I've written thirty-five thousand. Half a novel's worth. Perhaps I'll end up showing it to agent Deborah one day.

BP 136 over 91 (normal).

12th October

Another month seems to have passed and still no word on *Nimrod*. Call from Deborah who tells me she's spoken to the publishers but no decision has been made. The boss still hasn't read it. I hoped he would before Frankfurt. Clearly failed to do that as Frankfurt is this week and we haven't heard anything back. Deborah tells me it's symptomatic of the way publishing is at the moment, but then, worryingly, mentions that Tasja felt there was more work to be done on the novel before she wanted to publish it. I think she half expected me to offer to do the work before they made a commitment to it but I didn't. So I wait and seethe, remembering the final draft was delivered to Deborah on 4 June.

This month marks the first birthday of the *An American Cockroach* screenplay. Meeting last week with PYD at the new club run by The Ivy. Three posh floors, a young French doorman in a uniform and a glass staircase. All very nineties. Goujons of fish (seven pieces) for £12; you also get a pot of tartare sauce and half a lemon in a white gauze bag so when you squeeze it over the plaice the pips don't fall out. We discussed the latest draft of *Cockroach* and, as usual, he suggested that a number of changes are required, primarily in the first third which is currently a mess. After that it settles down. Nothing too drastic. He wants to put the accelerator down on the project. If he can get a draft of the script he's happy with he'll start sending it out to look for money. If all goes well it could be being shot next spring. I realise that recently I've been proceeding on the assumption that the constant redrafting is nothing more than an academic exercise and that the thing will never get made – but suddenly it becomes real again: I remind myself that the document on my hard drive (labelled 'Cockroach_2b') is actually a film script and one day it might be made into a film. Films do occasionally get made from scripts written by writers like me.

Also heard back from Fay on the other new screenplay, *Home*, which she liked but had a couple of issues with the tone, now rectified. She tells me a new production company has seen *Ivan and the Dead Guy* and wants to see me. They don't, of course, want to produce it but are keen to meet me for a producer/head-cold-type meeting. They're in Soho so I can wander over there one lunchtime. Reread *Ivan* the other day and still convinced there's something in it, but now see it's a bit of a mess tonally (usual problem). At the moment it's two films – the tragi-comic relationship between Ivan (a trainee medic working in an NHS hospital), a dying boy (Simon) and a corpse (Guy), and the police plot – which is absurdist. The piece would work better without the absurdist sub-plot so I'll revisit that one.

25th October

Tasja emailed me at the end of last week to tell me she'd finally made the offer on *Nimrod* to Deborah, but didn't tell me what it was. She was very happy they were going to publish the novel. It was late in the afternoon so I immediately called Deborah to find out what the offer was. She was in a meeting. I asked her to call me back urgently. She didn't. The following morning I texted her at 8 a.m. to tell her I really wanted to hear what Portobello had offered and could she call me at the office. No call by 11 so I called her assistant to be told she had been frantically trying to reach me. Obviously not, however, by phone, mobile phone or email. Having heard nothing by 12.15 I went out for lunch. When I got back still no message. I chased her for much of the afternoon, finally reaching her just before I was due to go home. She apologised and said she'd been hiding and too ashamed to call me. She'd been wondering how to break the offer to me – £1000 for world rights. 'There,' she said. 'I was wondering how to tell you and I ended up just blurting it out.' In a career of low points a new low point has been reached. I can't, of course, accept it. Luckily Tasja is away for next week so we don't have to respond straight away. It's a shame, really, I like Portobello and I like Tasja. She worked very hard on the last novel. I suspect, however, that her enthusiasm for my work wasn't shared by others in the company so it's time for this literary stealth bomber to try elsewhere. *Publishing rule 16: A common rejection strategy used by publishers is to make an offer so low that the writer is obliged to turn it down. That way both publisher and writer save face.*

On the positive side and maybe fortuitously, that day I'd had lunch with an old friend Andreas who now works as a commissioning editor at Constable & Robinson. He asked what I was up to and I mentioned my current frustrations with the lengthy wait for an offer. We talked a bit about strategies and he said that if he was publishing me he'd have some strong ideas about which part of the market to target my work. He also said it was important to remember that I was a good writer and I shouldn't forget that. Made me realise that the last few years have undoubtedly knocked my confidence to the extent that I now wonder if I have any talent whatsoever. I decided to send him a copy of the manuscript of *Nimrod* just for interest.

When I learned of the offer from Portobello I emailed him to suggest that if he meant what he said about my writing perhaps he could read the manuscript with a view to making an offer on it. A glimmer of hope. I then emailed Deborah to tell her, assuming she might be annoyed that I'd taken matters into my own hands. Email by return to tell me she'd been discussing the dismal offer with another agent at her company and they'd been talking about where else they could try *Nimrod*. Andreas' name was the first one the other agent mentioned. She likes him and considers him an intelligent and energetic young publisher with a good independent company. So the submission has her blessing.

Latest missive back from PYD who feels that the latest draft of *Cockroach* has some good points and some bits that don't work. I emailed back to say that as far as I was concerned the script was fine from act two onwards but act one was still all over the place. I suggested he could maybe concentrate on the first fifty pages and leave the rest alone for the time being. A day later he emailed back to say he'd followed my advice and felt act one was now much stronger as he's reinstated some of the stuff we'd removed from earlier drafts. He's also written in a couple more scenes. He's going to live with it for a few more days before sending it back for what must now be draft eleven or twelve – or twenty.

All in all, then, not quite the result I'd been hoping for on either project. I suppose I should be grateful that there are still people who continue to be bothered to engage with my writing. I know a number of writers who started publishing when I did and have now given up because they could no longer stand the pain.

3rd November

A school reunion in Derbyshire at the weekend. An old friend – always reliably blunt – announced that he'd tried to read my second novel – *Deserters*. 'It was,' he explained to me, 'about some poofs in Brighton' but he 'couldn't be doing with it.' He gave up three-quarters of the way through. 'Bloody rubbish, it was,' he concluded before heading back to the bar. Evening otherwise very convivial.

A week now since Andreas has had the manuscript of *Nimrod*. Tasja is back from half-term today so will presumably be expecting a response to her offer. I'm supposed to be having lunch with agent Deborah today. I slightly regret an email I sent last week. It was in response to one from the head man at Portobello. He'd circulated a job advert to all the authors on his list suggesting that they might be interested in it. The UEA are looking for a published writer to lecture on their creative writing course. I emailed back to thank him and to add that with the advances that they were offering nowadays a reasonably paid day job was a necessity for their writers. Smallminded, I know, and not surprised to get no response, not even 'Goodbye'.

PYD emailed the first sixty pages back on *Cockroach* with great enthusiasm. He's added a few scenes and reinstated quite a lot of his dialogue that I'd taken out. I emailed back to suggest that it seemed fine but I wanted to go through it and tweak it again. Got a slightly wounded email back by return. I think he expected my response to be much more positive. I think he feels the script is now ready to go out to the inner circle for further discussion but to my mind there are still too many lines in it that I'm not happy to put my name to. Tricky one. I suggested we meet to discuss all the lines I was unhappy with so I could offer him an explanation. Otherwise the process could go on forever, with me removing his new lines, sending them back to him, and him reinstating them. He replied to say he'd like to go through the final fifty pages and then send me the whole script to look at. Perhaps I should just let it go now, agree all the changes and wait and see if we can get the money.

So the two remaining projects – novel and film – which both looked positive a month back now hang in the balance. By the end of this week one of them might be resolved one way or the other but I'm now concerned for *Nimrod*. If this one isn't published I think I'll pack it in – after all that will be nearly three novels which haven't found a home and I can't face another one being rejected.

My season ticket runs out in two weeks' time and I've decided to attempt to commute to work on my new Vespa scooter (I passed the motorbike test two weeks ago so can now ride a larger bike and use the motorways). It's fifty-five miles each way so a fairly lengthy journey but, having commuted for nearly twenty-eight years, I'm not sure I can face another year of overcrowded trains, mobile phone conversations and vast expense. This will have implications for my writing but I hope the scooter might get me home quicker so I'll have more time to write when I get there. Or perhaps I'm subconsciously creating a situation that will make it more difficult for me to find time for writing so I can pack it in without feeling too bad about it. It is, after all, tough to write novels and hold down a day job. I would have liked at one point in my life to have earned enough to write full time – I don't think anybody can reach their potential until they've tried it without the distraction of full-time employment. But it was just not to be.

Later: Deborah cancelled lunch but called to tell me she intended to speak to Tasja at Portobello and to Andreas at Constable. She promised to call me back to tell me the results of the calls but no call by close of play.

I emailed PYD to ask about progress on latest draft of

Cockroach and got an email back from him as soon as I'd pressed send. We'd emailed each other at exactly the same moment. For the time being at least we're in psychic harmony. I'll have a look at the draft over the next day or so. He's keen to get it out there to his trusted inner circle and his agent.

This week's *TLS* includes a column from Hugo Williams recounting his London Palladium outing to see an Ian Fleming/*James Bond* extravaganza in aid of the British Heart Foundation. It prompted him to quote Fleming's advice to writers never to go back over what they have written. 'If you once look back you are lost. How could you have written this drivel? By following my formula you can write two thousand words a day and not be disgusted with them until the novel is finished.' Must pass on this advice to PYD.

6th November

Finally PYD and I have agreed a draft of *An American Cockroach* we're both happy to subscribe to so he's sent it off to his agent to get a response. Email from Fay to tell me the third payment is due on it so another £1500 (ish). She also asks me for a couple of dates she can offer to the film company who want to see me (head-cold/posters-on-the-floor-type meeting). I suggested next Monday or Friday. I ask her if there was any progress on the new screenplay, *Home*, but she's got a reading day on Friday and will get to it then.

Emailed Andreas at Constable to alert him to the fact that agent Deborah might call to formalise the submission of *Nimrod*. He emailed back to say they'd talked and 'If I can do it here I definitely will.' So that just leaves the tricky issue of whether or not he likes it. Deborah then called in the early evening to report on a conversation with Tasja. Seems they can't understand her shock at the offer. I asked her to check the original email to make sure it didn't say £10,000 or £100,000 instead of £1000 but no, definitely £1000. It's a record for Deborah's agency apparently but not one I should be proud to hold – the lowest offer they've ever had on a book. At least I'll be remembered for something.

10th November

Jury still out on *Nimrod* and *Cockroach*. Both are now at a crucial stage. Publisher Andreas is meeting Deborah this week to discuss *Nimrod*, at which point an offer might be made. I don't, however, know which day they're meeting so the call might come at any moment. *Cockroach* is being read by PYD's agent, at which point the decision will be made as to whether to send it out to try and get a production company and/or talent attached.

The season ticket runs out on 19 November. This means that there's a possibility that this will be my last week of commuting by train. I think the chances of scootering up and back to work every day of the year are rather slim, it's a round trip of 110 miles, but it has to be worth a try. One of the carriage regulars has a new phone which has a profoundly annoying text alert: 'Incoming' it begins in a helium voice, followed by the sound of a missile exploding and a laugh. It's very loud.

Meeting arranged for this Friday lunchtime with a film company in Soho so, all in all, a busy week writing-wise.

17th November

Some progress on a couple of fronts but no resolution on anything yet. I emailed PYD on Saturday to ask if we'd had a response from his agent on *Cockroach*. Turns out he's not read it yet but was due to read it over the weekend so there may be news today. No word from Deborah on the meeting with Andreas about *Nimrod* so I emailed Andreas to ask if he'd met up with her. He reports that he had and they got on very well. He hasn't finished *Nimrod* yet but will do this week. 'It promises very well,' he says and repeats that if he can do it he definitely will. I spend the following hour wondering if 'it promises very well' is a strong enough declaration of interest.

Last Friday lunchtime the latest film producer/head-cold meeting. It took place in a small sinister cul-de-sac close to Berwick Street market in Soho. As I turned into the street I could see a man in the shadows at the far end lying prone on the floor being kicked in the head by another man. A chef in scruffy whites, loitering and smoking outside the back door of his kitchen, was looking on impassively. A few steps further in I saw a film crew hidden behind a van, filming the scene. The film company's office was next door to the ground floor entrance to a flat on which a note was pinned: 'Model, Please ring.' As I rang on my bell, a man rang on the model's door and was let in. I didn't glimpse the model.

It took a while for my ring to be answered. A dusty reception area was visible through the dirty glass of the door. It looked as though it had never been staffed. There were two bicycles propped against the desk. After a third ring of the bell a cheerful young woman appeared and let me in, apologising that she'd been at the top of the building. I followed her through the empty, cold reception area and she then diverted into a small kitchen cupboard, offering me a coffee. I accepted. She said she wasn't much good at making coffee (it was instant, no milk or sugar, so there wasn't a great deal of culinary skill involved). She then led the way upstairs into a rented office which looked like the drawing room of a retired sea captain. Dominating the room a couple of large oil paintings of galleons in full sail at war, against one wall a Chinese lacquered cabinet sporting a mounted piece of plank (from the *Victory* I think), and at the centre of the room a large, circular oak table. On one of the walls was a large framed poster of the company's latest film – which, being a British film, was one I hadn't seen. The company, according to the female producer, had, however, got a good track record. She reeled off four recent big films they'd made, all of which I'd heard of, and one of which she apologised for (quite rightly if the reviews are to be believed). They also made the film in which (as a friend described), 'James Bond did the woman from *Dinnerladies* up the wrong'un.'

The producer went on by announcing she'd read four of my scripts and said she very much liked the writing. I thanked her. She referred to her notes throughout. On each script she'd written a lengthy report on yellow paper. She was flattering about the dialogue and characterisation, singling out *Ivan* and *Home*, suggesting she liked them but felt both had plot flaws. I agreed. We talked and I mentioned I was keen to revisit *Ivan*, to focus it more on the relationship between the medical student and the terminal boy. She said she'd very much like to see it when I'd rewritten it and I should email her if I wanted to discuss progress. No money on the table but genuine interest. She has a meeting this week with the Film Council. Her company has been shortlisted for some development funding so they might be able to put some funding into projects if they get it.

At the weekend I put down a few thoughts and have decided I'll spend the next few weeks knocking *Ivan* into shape, by which time there might be a verdict on *Nimrod* and possibly some progress on *Cockroach*. All in all some good things in prospect.

24th November

No verdict on *Nimrod's Shadow* yet. I emailed Andreas this morning and he asked for another week as a couple of his projects have gone awry. I said there was no rush. Eight months now since it was finished.

Ivan is progressing well. About three-quarters of the way through now and more scenes with Ivan and the terminal boy. Holding together well. Emailed producer L. to tell her and to ask how the Film Council meeting went. Seems it went poorly as they always do. They asked her to define what a British film was. I could have answered. It's a film starring Clive Owen or Keira Knightley which nobody bothers to go and see because there are too many words in it and no jokes. It will have been part funded by the BBC and set in the Second World War or the fifties. Bill Nighy is also likely to play second lead. Which brings me to *Cockroach*.

Cockroach is at last ready to go. Huge joy and relief. PYD sent me the latest draft yesterday afternoon. I tweaked it and sent it back. He was very positive in his response and says the first port of call for the script will be Daniel Craig (not, interestingly, Clive Owen). All sounds rather pie in the sky, but then he did attract several major stars to be in his last movie so perhaps there is a chance he'll get it off the ground. In his email he said he'd much enjoyed our collaboration and apologised for it being frustrating. I emailed back to say that it had been tough but I had enjoyed it. Which I have, mostly, so far. He signed off by inviting me to The Ivy tomorrow for wine and whisky 'To celebrate some really great work', and concluding 'Let's get this film made.'

Maybe, just maybe, this will be the one.

4th December

Ivan draft two is now off to the new production company and *Cockroach* is hopefully now out in the world though PYD is in LA so will be off the radar for a few days. He is taking his boxing gloves as he knows there's a gym local to where he's staying.

After a convivial lunch with him last Friday I asked Fay to invoice PYD for the final tranche of the option payment assuming that my work, for now, was finished. Arrived home to find a rather angry email forwarded from her from PYD which announced that the final payment wasn't due as the final draft hadn't been completed. He was owed at least one more draft. Further, he didn't welcome being 'charged for his time'. Entirely my fault as I somehow misunderstood where we were. The line between rewrites and tweaks is a fine one, especially when you're working fairly informally as we have been doing. He concluded by suggesting that we continue the project in the spirit with which it has been conducted so far. I emailed back explaining that it was my mistake and yes we should keep up the good spirit. Leaves a rather nasty taste in the mouth and rather spoils what should have been a good day.

No news yet on *Nimrod*. The extra time Andreas asked for expires today.

11th December

Postscript on *Cockroach*. Email from PYD late afternoon to declare that his agent felt the latest draft was 'very strong' and had already sent it to an independent producer in New York. I looked her up on the internet and saw that she was regarded as the twenty-fifth of the fifty most powerful people in the independent movie business. She has worked with Ang Lee. Emailed Fay to tell her. She replied that as the script had been sent out we should assume that the script is, therefore, finished and so the final bit of the fee was due so why did PYD seem so annoyed last week? She confirmed that the indie producer was well respected and had a good track record of working with newish directors. Wonder if she feels the same about newish writers, particularly the 1001st most important UK and Commonwealth writer (living)? My ranking should definitely improve should this get made. I award myself two hundred places and now consider myself the 801st most important writer (living).

17th December

Slightly nauseous this morning following the annual agent's party last night. I left at 9 p.m. feeling I'd been there for hours but actually it was only an hour and a half. Fairly gloomy atmosphere due perhaps to the credit crunch. Several *Daily Telegraph* hacks were collected in a huddle by the booze table discussing which of them had been fired. The *Independent* is due to announce cuts before Christmas. Met up with a few writers I hadn't seen since last year, all of whom seemed to have had a very good year. One wrote a mega-selling non-fiction book and won prizes, another has just signed a decent contract with a major hardback publisher who loves his new novel. His last one has just been turned into a play and is garnering fantastic reviews in Europe. Apparently it's going down very well in Russia. He asks about me and I fill him in. 'The point is,' he says, 'we're both good writers. But it's just the luck of the draw whether you find a publisher and sell.' Although it's not the time for business talk I do ask Deborah if she's heard from Andreas about *Nimrod*. The extra week he asked for has now turned into three weeks. But no news apparently, though she did rather sheepishly mention he'd popped in last week to see another agent and it was obvious she hadn't spoken to him when he came in.

Trudged home gloomily feeling less than optimistic over my literary career. It feels like a long journey to Brighton by tube and train on a winter's night as the chill reaches into your bones as you slowly sober up. Sleep is to be avoided on the 11.33 p.m. semi-fast to the coast because you might, as a friend did, wake in a freezing cold carriage in a railway siding near Haywards Heath just after 3 a.m.

No news on *Cockroach* or *Ivan* by the way. Only a week to Christmas so it seems unlikely there will be any more developments this year.

19th December

Finally, after some prompting, a response from Andreas to *Nimrod*. Not quite the response I'd hoped. He turned it down. Not, he said, because he didn't like it. He said he felt it was the most commercial of my books. However, his publishing house has been looking at the figures for next year and are not getting into literary fiction. Feeling somewhat deflated by this I emailed agent Deborah to suggest that perhaps it was time for me to look around elsewhere for an agent too, to start the new year on a clean sheet. She'd done enough for me and it was only fair on her for me to move on. She immediately phoned. Told me not to be ridiculous and said that if she felt she was no longer the right agent for me then there would be somebody else there who would take me on. I said it was perhaps time for me to have a face-to-face with Tasja at Portobello. If they genuinely believe they can do something with the book then maybe it's best we just get on with it and sod the risible advance. She agreed it was worth a meeting. So I emailed Tasja and said that I was concerned the offer from them reflected their enthusiasm. She said it definitely did not. That they were still interested in publishing good books despite the dire times. That the marketing person loved it and that she wanted to meet in January to talk. So that's what we're doing.

Meanwhile Fay emailed to ask if I'd be interested in being put up to adapt a novel into a screenplay. Sounded interesting so I said yes, put me in the mix (chances of me getting it are of course zero but I go through the motions). I then emailed PYD to wish him seasonal greetings and suggest we catch up in the new year. He emailed back to say several people were reading *Cockroach* and that he intended to give it to Daniel Craig in January. He was, he said, on a beach in Costa Rica. In fact the first line of his email (which must have come from his Blackberry) was 'On a beach in Costa Rica.'

And finally an email from L. on *Ivan*. She has not read it as she has a film just about to be delivered and a finance deal to sort out. She will read it over Xmas and we'll speak in January. So that's about it for 2008 I think. Another frustrating year but maybe a few green shoots of recovery. Here's to 2009.

Part 2

A hospital journal

'Withnail is right. We are indeed drifting into the arena of the unwell.'

Bruce Robinson

2009

And then everything changed. In the early hours of Sunday 11 January I was admitted to hospital with what the A&E doctor suspected was appendicitis. It wasn't. It proved to be something more serious – diverticulitis with complications, the subsequent treatment of which I recorded in a notebook supplied by Julie a couple of days into what would prove a lengthy hospital stay. She said I'd want to make a note of what was happening to me. I said I wouldn't. She was, of course, right.

The entries in the journal are random and undated. Some are transcripts of overheard conversations, some from dreams or vivid memories. All influenced by the regular imbibing of morphine to keep the agony at bay. As time went on, dates ceased to have any meaning as did the differentiation between night and day.

The first entry was made when I overheard the man in the bed next to mine talking to a nurse. I labelled him Detox Dave (the names of all those I encountered have been changed). He was one of the many alcoholics on the 'Digestive Diseases' floor. When we first talked Detox Dave confessed that before being admitted to be detoxed he was drinking over three hundred units a week. He kept most of us awake at night because he couldn't sleep due to the detox. He was a thin, wounded, rat-like man with a long knife scar that ran from just beneath his right eye to his lip. I had little sympathy for him. But my sympathy grew when I overheard a nurse interviewing him behind the curtain one afternoon.

Detox Dave 1

The nurse: 'I'm going to ask you some questions, OK?'

Dave: 'OK.'

'Where do you live?'

'Basement flat.'

'On your own?'

'Yeah.'

'Private or council?'

'Private.'

'Do you get any help?'

'No.'

'What about your parents?'

'No. I don't know if you saw my dad yesterday when he came in; the way he was dressed. He's a very successful businessman. He's away a lot. My mum can't help. She's ill. She's got colitis.'

'How long have you been like this?'

'2005 I started to get suicidal.'

'We can't deal with that. You need to talk to the mental health team for that. I'm just trying to assess your physical needs. What issues would you say you deal with?'

'Depression, low self-esteem, can't see a future.'

'Anything good? Anything positive?'

'My relationship gone wrong. My son. I don't see him. Self-harming. That's about it really.'

'OK.'

Night 1

At 3.15 a.m., nearly twenty-four hours since my arrival at A&E, a surgeon arrives at my bedside to tell me that the scheduled operation will not take place until the following morning. There have been two emergencies and the team are tired. He prescribes morphine for the pain and wishes me a good night's sleep.

Day 2, morning, pre-operation

At 9 a.m. a young, smiling, consultant anaesthetist arrives, kneels beside my bed and shakes my hand.

'I'll be looking after you,' he tells me. 'I've talked to the surgical team and I agree an operation is necessary. You have my word I will be watching you very closely. There will be a good outcome. Do you have any concerns?'

I tell him about a work colleague who underwent a caesarean and felt every incision of the knife.

'OK, that's a genuine concern,' he concedes. 'I can give you something that will remove short-term memory. Would you like me to do that?'

'That sounds good.'

'Don't worry. It will be fine.' He stands agilely on enviably painless knees. 'Just one thing.'

'Yes?'

'The last thing you might feel before we put you out is my hands round your throat. You might feel as if you are being strangled.'

'. . . OK.'

'This is to prevent the contents of your stomach rising up into your mouth. But don't worry.'

Later, when I am taken down I have a vague memory of a face looming over me and hands reaching towards my throat.

Recovery

I don't remember waking after the operation or the five hours in recovery. A result perhaps of the drug I have ingested to remove short-term memory. The next thing I am aware of is the sudden arrival of a consultant and a group of medical students at my bedside and the consultant announcing to me and to his audience that it wasn't appendicitis, as they had suspected, but diverticulitis. Diverticula are small sacs that protrude from weak points in the intestines like bulges in a bicycle tyre. Most Westerners over fifty have them and live without them causing any problems. However, on rare occasions, they become infected and rupture.

'There was some infected bowel so we took out about two inches and stapled you back together,' the consultant confirms. 'We found nothing else nasty in there. Slightly more complicated than we anticipated but you should be fine. OK?'

'Thanks.'

'Any questions?'

'Can I have something for the pain?'

I learn later from Julie that following the operation she was called on her mobile phone and it was suggested she get herself promptly to the hospital. She was also advised to bring my daughter from work and my son from school. They were, of course, terrified, fearing the worst. When they learned about the diverticulitis they were relieved. Their relief was greater than the anger they later felt.

Without them, their daily visits and reassurances, the ordeal would have been beyond endurance. In this new context I see my children in a different light. My daughter is a woman now; capable and caring and strong. My son shakes my hand quite warily when he visits. At seventeen it's hard for him to show what he feels but I can see he's concerned for me. He enjoys being given tasks when he comes in – repair the bedside TV, change the batteries in the radio. We hug when he leaves. I weep copiously; tears of terror and sadness.

The Ghost 1

I meet The Ghost on my third or fourth or fifth night. I can't sleep. It's 2.20 a.m. The morphine and the after-effects of the anaesthetic are making me hallucinate so I go down in the lift to stand outside in the open air, just beyond the tower block doors. It's below freezing but I can't feel the cold. I am attached to a metal stand on which my morphine supply and various liquids hang like fruit from the branches of a leafless tree. The Ghost – a young, athletic-looking man – is standing just outside the door, smoking. He is wearing a black dressing gown and a black fur ushanka hat, earpieces tied above his head. He too has a metal stand with two bags of fluids attached to it. He has a stoma bag attached to the wound at the centre of his belly, visible through the opening in his dressing gown. The bag is semi-transparent and I can see that it is full of straw-coloured liquid.

'All right, mate?' he asks.

'Not bad.'

'Can't sleep?'

'No.'

'Me neither. What you in for?'

'I came in for appendicitis but they found diverticulitis.'

'Same here, mate. Feel for you. Then I got adhesions. Been in and out of here for nine months. I've got a fistula. Can't drink. Nil by mouth. When you going out?'

'Soon. Next day or so they said.'

'Good luck, mate.'

'And you.'

John Terry

The first few days post-op are spent on a ward I learn is called 'Beirut'. Beirut is a high-intensity ward in which three nurses serve six patients. This is where the seriously ill and the immediate post-op patients reside. I am in the middle bed on the right-hand side. Alcoholic Alan occupies the bed closest to the door against the left-hand wall. Next to him and directly facing me is a dying man. The curtains around his bay are closed and throughout the night distraught relatives arrive to bid him farewell. An elderly man with cancer is in the bed next to his. To my right is a cadaverous man in his sixties who keeps taking off his gown and displaying his genitals to the nurses. Another liver patient. His conversation and behaviour are infantile. He doesn't sleep but spends all night calling out 'John Terry, John Terry, John Terry.' Occasionally a nurse comes to ask him to be quiet. The curtain to my left is half closed so I can't see the top half of the body of my neighbour – another liver patient. I can, however, see his white shins and purple feet. A surgeon and a nurse occasionally attend to him, using what looks like an electric razor on the skin. The smell is appalling.

At a little after 4 a.m. the man behind the curtain dies. Death, I come to learn, is a regular, sometimes welcome, visitor here. I hear the sudden outpouring of grief. More relatives arrive. Some leave. The ward is flooded with the smell of conflicting perfumes. The body is removed two hours later to the accompanying chant of 'John Terry, John Terry, John Terry.'

The wound explodes

3 a.m. and Beirut is busy. It's a male-only ward but because of capacity problems on the sister ward a woman has just been wheeled into the bay next to mine after an operation. Several nurses attend to her. She moans and screams in pain. I can't sleep anyway – the hallucinations are getting worse. I have not slept for several nights and am watching *News 24* but I can't find a position of comfort. I feel sick. My temperature is high and the morphine no longer seems to be taking the edge off the pain in the lower right-hand side of my stomach. Evidently somebody has opened me up and stitched a melon and several razor blades inside me. I reach for my wound. It feels wet. I touch my fingers to my nose and smell bile. To get away from the noise and chaos of the ward I take my fluid stand to the lavatory and tentatively raise my pyjama jacket. Thick green fluid is pouring down my stomach from the stapled wound. It smells rank. I vomit and pull the alarm cord. A nurse arrives, inspects the mess, gently tells me not to worry and guides me back to bed. She will call a doctor. I vomit again. The doctor arrives, instructs the nurse to send me for an X-ray and tells her to 'tube' me.

A porter arrives and takes me on a surreal night-time journey along cold, low-lit, empty hospital corridors. I am shivering uncontrollably. The X-ray technician is busy with another emergency but she emerges a little after 4 a.m. and I am taken into a cold room filled with ice-blue light. I am asked to stand against a metal plate. I do so with difficulty. The porter delivers me back to the ward. The gentle Filipino nurse is waiting for me. She pulls the curtains round my bay and tells me I am to have a tube inserted into my stomach.

'This will not be nice,' she cautions. 'But you must work with me and it will be easier. OK, darling?'

'OK.'

'So what I am going to ask you to do is to take a sip of this water and hold it in your mouth. When I say swallow, please swallow. When you swallow I will feed this white tube up your nostril. It will then go down your throat and eventually into your stomach. OK?'

'. . . OK.'

'This will drain your stomach so your bowel can have a nice rest for a while.'

I sip and hold and feel the sharp tube entering my nose. I swallow and feel the tube in my throat. I retch. She tells me to take another sip and hold it, then swallow. She feeds in more tube and four sips and swallows later the drain is in place. I vomit again – the tube at the back of my throat is making me gag. But this time the vomit issues from the tube into a bag which is now attached to the side of my bed. Over the following four days the contents of my ailing stomach drain into this bag, occasionally aided by a nurse who attaches a syringe to the tube to help them on their way. The contents of the stomach are green, the consistency and colour of plankton. My bowel, meanwhile, is taking a well-earned rest.

Barrel Man

Barrel Man arrives on the ward early one evening. He is truly extraordinary. His legs are white and spindly but his belly is the shape of a beer barrel. His belly button extends some four or five inches from his stomach like a baby's arm. He was brought in because the Meals on Wheels service alerted the police that his door had remained unanswered for two days. The police broke in and immediately called an ambulance. This elderly man is a former alcoholic and his liver is not functioning – his stomach now holds many litres of liquid.

Barrel Man is immediately put on a drain. Several bags of clear fluid are emptied from his stomach every couple of hours. During the night, around 2 a.m., we hear the sound of a cry and a splash of liquid. Barry (in the bed opposite to mine – we're around the same age but he calls me 'young man' – he's very tough) presses his bell. The room fills with the aroma of faeces. A nurse dashes in, switches on the light and pulls Barrel Man's curtain round, but not before we have glimpsed the pool of blood and faeces on the floor. The nurse dashes out. Two doctors arrive. Barrel Man is wheeled down to theatre. We don't expect to see him on the ward again. With typical understatement, the following day the nurse reports his condition as 'very poorly'.

Detox Dave 2

For an hour one afternoon Detox Dave goes AWOL then reappears with two Morrisons carrier bags from which he takes out two bottles of Ribena. Many of the alcoholics here are street sleepers in waiting, clinging on to their bedsits or local authority flats by their fingernails. Dave calls across the ward to his new best friend, ward mate Baz.

'Got some Ribena, mate. Two bottles. Got some ice. Here, mate, sort yourself a jug. Here, have a jug, mate. Got myself two salads from Morrisons: prawn and chicken. Gonna put them in the fridge and put stickers on them with my name on. Here, mate, have a Ribena if you want one.'

Detox Dave sits on his bed and dials a number on his mobile phone.

'Hello, mate, I've just seen your ad in the *Friday Ad* for the Nokia. You still got it? . . . Yeah, only the thing is I'm in hospital . . . £40? Can you get it here? I'm very interested . . . Yes, mate. Ninth floor. Tower block. About seven? Sweet.'

Dave calls across the room to Barry.

'He's got one of them Nokias fully boxed. Wants forty for it. I'll offer him a dirty thirty. Worth £200 that is.'

Fistula

The day after the wound explodes I learn that the crisis was caused by an enterocutaneous fistula – a tear in the bowel at the site of the operation. The bowel vented its contents into the stomach. It happened because as the wound in the bowel join began to heal the scar tissue attached itself to the back of the stomach lining. When the bowel moved it adhered to the stomach and a hole was torn. The good news is that the fistula is draining directly to the wound site and not into my stomach, otherwise another urgent operation would have been needed. On the morning ward round the consultant instructs the nurse to remove five staples from the wound to allow it to open up and put a stoma bag over the open wound to collect the contents. These are to be monitored over a twenty-four-hour period.

Around 800 ml drains on the first day. The smell of it is indescribably rank but the nurses claim not to be able to smell it and go about the emptying with cheery efficiency. The hope is that the fistula will slowly heal itself. The healing will be signalled by a reduction in the output into the bag. If it doesn't another operation will be necessary. I ask the consultant what this will entail. 'Just a simple operation to sew up the hole?' I suggest.

'Not quite. We'd need to go in and take out a further section of the bowel – about a foot, then resection it. We'd like to avoid that if we can.'

So would I.

The Ghost 2

It's pointless trying to sleep because of the hallucinations so I continue to wander the corridors at night. Again, sometime between midnight and dawn, I meet The Ghost who expresses surprise that I am still in there and asks: 'How you doing, mate?'

'Fistula.'

'Shit. That's what I got. I feel for you, mate. You got a bag?'

'Yes.'

'What's it doing?'

'800 ml today.'

'Mine was doing about that at the beginning but they sent me home. It kept pissing out all over my clothes and me and my missus had to come up here on the bus in the middle of the night. I had eight bags on this. Stinks, doesn't it?'

'Yes.'

'I feel for you, mate. I really do. I used to be a boxer. I was fit. I can't fight now. I got a window-cleaning round but that's gone to shit too.'

Swimming to the pier

I have lost all track of time. Days blur into nights. I have tried to explain to my wife that I have been in this hospital before, for a similar operation two years ago, but she assures me this is the first time. I know she is wrong. My sanity is straining at the leash. I can't sleep because each time I close my eyes I fall into the same hellish dream. I am walking along a corridor – I think it is the rough-walled corridor in the local cinema which leads from the foyer to the auditorium. As I walk I stumble but when I fall to the floor I roll over, head over heels, again and again. I roll faster and faster and faster, hitting every jagged surface I pass. I put out my hands but I can't stop myself. The agony is immense. Finally I hit a wall and come to a halt. I am lying on my back and staring up at the sky and I know I have just experienced my death and am waiting for somebody to come and find my body. I have no doubt that this is how a brutal death will feel.

The same occurs every time I close my eyes. I have not slept now for many nights but at last I have found a solution to this mental turmoil. I will walk to the beach and I will swim out to sea. I want to feel the salt water on my body but I know that I will not feel the cold because the morphine will prevent it. The desire for the water against my skin is as fierce as a raging thirst. This hellish agony will be at an end. I plan my route. I will take the lift down to the sixth-floor exit (bizarrely, this is the ground floor – always open, the usual location of The Ghost). In the foyer I will detach my lines and morphine from the cannula in my arm and I will leave the fluid stand just outside the door. I will then walk down the slope, past the A&E car park and cross Eastern Road. The promenade is a short two- or three-minute walk down the hill. I will take the stone steps down from there and cross Madeira Drive to the beach, leave my pyjamas on the pebbles like Reginald Perrin and strike out to sea. I have no intention of drowning myself, no plans beyond swimming out towards the pier.

As I leave the ward I wink insanely at Barry. He is used to my nocturnal wanderings and retching and winks back. I've never seen him sleep.

'Have you ever swum in the sea?' I whisper.

'Yeah. I used to go every Christmas Day. Haven't done it for a few years though.'

The night sister is at the desk with one of the nurses, working with the aid of a cone of light from an anglepoise lamp.

'Where are you going?' she asks me.

'For some fresh air.'

'The nurse will come with you.'

'No, that's fine. Honestly. I can manage.'

'The nurse will come with you. We'd hate you to fall over . . . And hurt yourself.'

'. . . OK.'

Somehow the wise sister knows. The nurse comes outside with me. She tells me it's freezing cold but it seems perfectly warm to me. I return to bed and watch *Time Team* until the small hours. I am grateful when dawn breaks.

Morphine

A nurse arrives with what looks like a presentation wooden box with a glass lid. Inside it is a large, glistening syringe of morphine. The drug is connected directly to the cannula in my arm. To trigger the syringe I press a green illuminated switch. The light on the switch then goes out for a few minutes so I don't overdose. When it illuminates again I can administer another dose. I spend most of the day pressing the button and feeling like a member of Velvet Underground. Every hour a nurse arrives to check my pain score on a scale of one to ten. For most of the day I award it eight or nine, reserving full marks for some unimagined future horror.

Hallucinations

Ironically, on the Saturday I fell ill my wife and I were eating out with a friend and his wife who both work at this hospital. When I was admitted he texted to offer any support he could. I asked him to keep an eye on things. As a consultant I knew he'd be party to information that I wasn't. He was as good as his word. When the hallucinations showed no sign of abating and the consultant I was dealing with expressed no interest in them I texted my friend, pleading for his help. The following morning a doctor arrived at my bedside and asked what symptoms I was experiencing. I explained that every time I tried to sleep I was living through my own death and that this had been going on for five nights.

'Right. I'll prescribe a very nice drug for you. It's a very gentle sedative. I promise it will help you to sleep without the terror.'

I checked several times during the day that the drug

had been prescribed and had arrived on the ward. I was reassured several times that it had. That night at 10 o'clock I was given a tiny blue pellet and instructed to allow it to melt behind my tongue. I awoke with huge relief at 4 a.m. – nearly five hours' luxurious sleep. The first moments of peace since I was admitted.

Tea round

As a welcome break from the routine the daily tea round is much anticipated. It is conducted mid-afternoon by a Polish woman. She pilots an aluminium-coloured trolley from which she dispenses smiles, tea, coffee, chocolate, build-up drinks and biscuits from an old Quality Street tin. Today, however, being Sunday, the usual Polish woman is off and another, younger, Polish woman has taken her place. She is now standing at the foot of Kenneth's bed and peering at his whiteboard. Taking out a biro she writes something down on a paper napkin and takes it to the nurse checking Baz's blood pressure.

'Excuse me please, what is this?' The Polish woman proffers the napkin. The nurse takes it and reads it.

'"E and D". Eating and Drinking.'

'Eating and drinking?'

'Yes. He can eat and drink.'

'I see.' The Polish woman stands there for a moment longer looking blank. 'So he can have tea and/or coffee?'

'Yes.'

'And perhaps a biscuit?'

'Yes. He can eat and drink.'

'Thank you.'

Kenneth orders his usual hot chocolate and digestive, Baz a cup of coffee. The other three of us are on 'Sips', i.e., no fluids whatsoever, so nothing from the trolley. I have now eaten nothing for twenty-one days except half a bowl of jelly but I feel no hunger.

Detox Dave is visited

A shaven-headed youth arrives in a wheelchair from another ward to visit Detox Dave. They conduct a whispered conversation, in the course of which the youth asks Dave if he can 'sort him for some "wacky baccy"'.

'No, mate, I used to get mine from Lancing but they got raided.'

'OK. Well, you find any, you let me know.'

'Will do. I'm looking for some for personal.'

'I could do you some bennies.'

'No, mate, I don't do them no more.'

'Give me a bell if you're going down for a smoke and I'll meet you.'

'Sweet.'

'Bell me once and I'll come down.'

'Nice one.'

The wound

The wound is a tiny evil mouth in my stomach. Occasionally it belches and fluid plops out and into the stoma bag. This is accompanied by a burning sensation as the acid burns the skin.

An inconvenient truth

Nearly two feet of snow have fallen during the night. From the window I watch children sledging down the slope beside the barrack-like local authority flats that border the hospital site. It is now snowing heavily again.

Nurses visit the ward to look out of the window in wonder. The transport systems of the city are paralysed – there are no buses, taxis or trains.

'It's too cold to snow,' Detox Dave announces, despite the evidence to the contrary. 'I blame global warning. Nucular this, nucular that . . . I'm going to win the lottery so I can get some enjoyment. You going out for a fag, Baz? Wait for me.'

Julie arrives to visit me after walking for an hour and a half. She has not missed a day. She brings some phone photos she has taken of sheep which are grazing the school field next to our house. It feels like a place from a very distant past. After an hour's visit she walks the hour and a half back home.

Alcoholic Alan

Perhaps a third of the residents of the ninth floor are there because of liver problems caused by alcohol abuse. There's a debate on the TV about increasing the unit cost of alcohol to reduce the problem. Most of the alcoholics I've encountered in here spend between £500 and £800 a month on booze. These are not the well-heeled white-collar drinkers. An increase in cost I suspect would have little effect on their consumption.

I met Alcoholic Alan when I was in Beirut. He was in the bed closest to the door. His partner, who is some kind of trained healthcare assistant, took care of him: she changed the sheets, tried to feed him, tried to talk to him. She dispensed care with a tender brutality, whispering poisonous comments as she attended to him. Alcoholic Alan's skin is yellow. He never opened his eyes.

Three weeks later he still hasn't opened his eyes. His hair has been razored to his skull so he now looks like a Dickensian criminal tied to a poorhouse bed. His carer is looking wrecked from lack of sleep and fear. I overhear her talking to a nurse: 'He had three chances and he blew it. This is his fourth time in here.'

'You're coping with it very well.'

'Yeah, but I'll be in a puddle at the end.'

Alan purrs like a cat.

The following morning I pass Beirut Ward and Alan and his healthcare partner are gone. He died in the night. He was in his mid-thirties.

On my bedside table

Visitors are generous with both their time and gifts. Work colleagues have taken the trouble of coming down from London to see me for an hour. Libby made the journey from London and, ever keen for something to do, gleefully wheeled me to X-ray for one of my numerous appointments. I can't think of another radio presenter I've worked with who would go to the same trouble for their producer. My bedside table is testament to the generosity of the visitors. All have given thought to their gifts. I have six books: *I Once Met* (the collected *Oldie* columns), *Love and War in the Apennines* by Eric Newby, *The Black Swan* by Nassim Nicholas Taleb, *The Smithsonian Institute* by Gore Vidal, *Care of the Soul* by Thomas Moore and *The Paris Review Interviews Volume 3*. I have the *Spectator*, *New Statesman*, *Private Eye*, the *Simpsons* magazine, *Motorcycle News* and *Ride* magazine plus two copies of *Scootering*. The books are so far untouched, my concentration span currently approximately thirty seconds.

Nurses

It's a truism to suggest that nursing is a vocation but, having seen evidence of it at first hand, undoubtedly it is. The great majority of nurses who have looked after me have done so with compassion, tenderness and commendable efficiency. They have taken care of the physical needs but they have also been there at the dead of night with words of reassurance. They have emptied the foul contents of the stoma bag without revulsion, they conduct enemas on Barrel Man and somehow allow him to maintain his dignity. When I ask them why they do it and work relentless hours for such a pittance they tell me they couldn't imagine doing anything else. You can see in their eyes that they mean it.

Barrel Man rolls back

Barrel Man returns to the ward after a brief stay in Beirut. He is now biblically bearded, his hair long and rank. Both of his arms are tattooed with large purple bruises where they have tried to put in cannulas. He is barely conscious. He groans and coughs in his sleep. His stomach is significantly smaller than when he left.

My Baxter bag

I have had a picc line inserted into my arm and my nutritional needs are now being met from an aluminium-coloured bag on the metal stand beside my bed. The contents are delivered through a digital pump which regulates the flow. If air is detected in the line the pump bleeps an alarm. At night you can hear the metallic chirrups of the ward pumps delivering their goodness into veins. The contents of my Baxter bag are these:

Nitrogen: 13.2 g
Glucose energy: 1280 Kcal
LPID energy: 800 Kcal
Sodium: 64 mmol
Potassium: 48 mmol
Phosphate: 14 mmol
Calcium: 4 mmol
Magnesium: 4.4 mmol
Zinc: 153 umol
Selenium: 0.888 umol
Iron: 17.9 umol
Copper: 7.548 umol
Chloride: 96 mmol
Acetate: 144 mmol

The Baxter bag (plus another drip containing a litre of mixed potassium chloride and sodium chloride) is providing all my nutrition. Meantime, a couple of drains are plumbing away the infected fluids from my body into bags. I have not eaten anything for twenty-two days. The idea of food remains appealing but only abstractly. I feel no hunger.

How healing works

After four weeks' observation I can report that this is how I perceive the process of healing to be conducted:

The patient presents with symptoms. Bloods, X-rays and scans are taken, symptoms are analysed, a likely diagnosis made and a course of action arrived at.

Surgery is conducted, in the course of which the initial diagnosis is occasionally proved wrong and an alternative procedure is improvised.

The body reacts to this invasion by tormenting the patient with pain and swelling. If the surgery has been successful the pain and swelling reduce and the patient is sent home cured.

If this doesn't happen it's likely that some kind of infection has occurred. This is the body's way of alerting the consultant that they got it slightly wrong and now have to take further action – more surgery, antibiotics, other drugs, drains.

Infected matter pours from the site of the wound. This is monitored, as are all the patient's other vital signs (blood pressure, temperature, pulse, blood chemistry). A route map to health is formulated based on these signs. A dialogue has now been established between body and doctor – each reacting to the signals of the other.

Finally the body and the consultant reach an accommodation. When each understands the other the patient is on the road to recovery.

Clear fluids

Some time during week five the consultant announces that it's time to test the fistula by reintroducing clear fluids (black tea, coffee, squash, jelly, soup). If the fluids aren't immediately regurgitated into the stoma bag then the fistula has sealed. If the output to the bag diminishes or remains at its present 200 ml a day they'll introduce free fluids and then solids.

A cup of black coffee has now been delivered. I approach it with trepidation. I sip. It's not good coffee but it goes down and stays down and is not spat out from the evil little mouth in my side.

Bowels

This being the 'Digestive Diseases' floor bowels and the operation thereof provide an endless source of discussion. The term 'a regular guy' takes on a whole new meaning in here. When Barrel Man returned to the ward his first request was for a commode. When it was delivered he was soon calling out to the nurse that he had provided her with 'a lot of black stool'. The nurse emerged from his curtained cubicle bearing the sample at arm's length. We tend to present our samples to the nurses like proud schoolchildren bringing clay models home to our parents. They are always received with appreciation.

Flatulence here is considered a sign of improving health – often the first signal that a rested bowel is reawakening. Therefore any fart is unleashed loudly across the ward, usually earning spontaneous congratulations and words of encouragement – which is fine except, of course, when the practice continues during visiting times.

I have been farting like a wizard for two days now which means my bowel is waking up.

Drugs

In moments of boredom I look through my confidential folder to find out what they have written about me. The drugs chart lists what I have been given since I was first admitted: Warfarin, Heparin, Teds and Tinzaparin, Paracetamol, Citalopram, Chlorhexidine, Codeine, Gaviscon, Lansoprazole, Pabrinex, Oxcizine, Zopiclone, Lorazepam.

From my window

After leaving Beirut and moving to a side ward I have now (as ward senior) been awarded a coveted bed by a window.

From here I can see east directly across the Kemptown rooftops towards Roedean School. To the left of Roedean are visible the peaks of the Downs and the blue sky. Silhouetted against the skyline are the Bergman-esque figures of dog walkers. To the right is the marina. When the sea is high white curtains are thrown up and over the tall concrete barrier. The view is particularly good in the middle of the night when the roads are empty and the scene is lit by the sodium glow of the streetlights.

A seagull arrives each day at around 4 p.m. and taps its orange beak on the window. I provide it with a crust of bread I have taken from the breakfast scraps. When it has eaten it flies away.

If I look to my left at the building closest to this tower block I can see directly into the living room of a third-floor local authority flat. It is less than thirty yards away and the curtains are never drawn. Occasionally two young girls are in there playing darts. Today a young man is singing, accompanying himself on a Spanish guitar.

Alcoholic Alan's farewell

In the corridor I pass Alcoholic Alan's partner. Her eyes are black with grief and exhaustion. She can barely stand and is being supported by a friend. She has a huge carrier bag of boxes of budget fancy biscuits which she is dispensing to the nurses who made Alan's death more tolerable to her and, presumably, to him.

Detox Dave returns

Despite being discharged only twenty-four hours ago Detox Dave is back to visit Baz. As a gift he has brought him a party pack of prawn-cocktail-flavoured crisps.

He struts round the ward as if it was the scene of his greatest triumph and spends much of the visit demonstrating to Baz the operation of his new mobile phone. When he leaves I ask Baz how he is doing and Baz tells me that he'd had a couple of cans of strong lager that afternoon thus instantly rendering his five days of noisy detox on the ward completely fruitless.

Meanwhile a new alcoholic has been delivered to Beirut Ward. His screams can be heard from some distance away. Nurses emerge from his cubicle white-faced. He continues screaming for a few hours but falls silent around midnight.

The ward at night: 2.45 a.m., day?

The regular breathing of Barrel Man and the tinkling of pumps delivering liquids into veins breaks the silence of the night-time ward. Rain is being hurled at the window by a high westerly wind and a razor-sharp chill finds its way through the crack at the bottom. The cold is welcome. In the near distance I can see the fairground ribbon of lights on the coast road to Rottingdean and the traffic lights by the gasometers changing and changing – liquid green and amber and red spilling on to the wet road – while no cars wait. Occasionally a siren is heard and an ambulance arrives in A&E, blue lights capering round the surrounding buildings. Tonight there are also several police cars in the A&E car park.

I am afraid that I will remain in the arena of the unwell forever. The fear always returns at night. Earlier this evening The Ghost visited and announced that he was to have another operation. I see my future in him. I have been on clear fluids for two days now to test the fistula. I have had violent diarrhoea several times but the sister assures me this is perfectly normal.

Toast

The following morning's ward round is brisk. The consultant asks how I am. I tell him about the diarrhoea. He says he is not in the least bit concerned about that. 'You've gone through a critical two days. We'll put you on a light diet and get that TPN bag down. OK?'

'You mean I can eat again?'

'Yes. But just take it easy. Light diet. If all goes well you'll be out next week.'

After nearly six weeks in here the prospect is appealing.

The male nurse attending the ward round remains after the consultant and gaggle of students have departed, the curtains wafting in their slipstream.

'Good news, mate,' he says. He's a terrific bloke. A former builder who saw the light and changed career in his early twenties without a moment of regret.

'Yes.' I can't really process it.

'Do you want some toast? Marmalade? Marmite? Jam?'

'Toast and Marmite.'

'No worries. I'll get some for you.'

He delivers two slices of toast, warm from the small ward kitchen, two gold-wrapped pats of butter and a tiny plastic pod of Marmite. I contemplate the food for a while. I used to eat this stuff. Can I remember how? I spread the butter. The aroma of it melting into the slightly charred bread is intoxicating. I apply the Marmite with its glutinous resistance over the butter and pause to allow the smell to permeate my nostrils. Then I bite. I feel the soft abrasion of the toast against my raw palate, the soft comforting cloy of the butter coating my tongue and the sharp yeasty kick of the Marmite climbing my throat. I chew slowly. Another bite. Heaven. I can manage only one slice and I await my bowel's response to the first solids I have presented to it for many days.

Pain poker

Startled Nigel comes in badly bruised. He does, indeed, look startled, as if some sudden physical crime has been perpetrated against him. He is very well spoken, cadaverous, and has chosen to wear a nightshirt. Nightshirts are rarely tied correctly at the back and those who wear them tend to have their arses on display each time they leave their bed. He has tumours on his bladder and is another former alcoholic. Matt (another long-term resident) and I are discussing pain poker and Matt awards Startled Nigel the winning hand – the equivalent of a Royal Flush.

Low-value hands in pain poker (which are nevertheless worth risking a few pounds on) are: the insertion of a cannula, the insertion of a picc line, having bloods taken by an inexperienced phlebotomist, and the nightly injection into the stomach of the blood-thinning agent used to prevent DVT.

A slightly higher-valued hand is the needle into the wrist to draw out arterial bloods. This procedure involves a thick hypodermic syringe being plunged deep into the wrist and then waggled around until a deep vein is located. The initial insertion is fairly painful but the waggling around and fishing for a vein is agony – especially when administered by a junior doctor.

The third strongest hand is a colonoscopy which involves a camera being inserted into the rectum and then fed through the bowel. If this is done without pain relief, as it sometimes is, the pain becomes troublesome when the camera has to find a way through a turn in the interior pipework and the operator has to shove it a bit harder.

The second is the insertion of a line into the nostril and down the throat to drain the stomach (see above).

But the winning hand is the ordeal Startled Nigel has just undergone. This was a cystoscopy which involved a tube with a tiny scalpel on the end being inserted into his urethra. 'Shocking and terrifying,' he reported the experience to be. We can think of nothing worse and, with applause, gladly award him the top prize.

Barrel Man's story

Barrel Man has been returned to the bed opposite mine. He is talking more and sleeping less but still seems confused. He tells me that until recently he lived with his mother. His health problems are the result of his alcoholism. Although he has not drunk anything for almost a year he is now living with the effects of the twelve years during which he drank a bottle of gin a day. He has sclerosis of the liver. They had hoped it would regenerate when he stopped drinking but it's too badly damaged. It's unlikely he will be offered a transplant because of his age and he has been told he will probably die within three months. His mother is in a nursing home and he has yet to phone her and give her the news. He is never visited. The character that emerges is that of a gentle, rather melancholic and solitary man. He never complains, deals with the nurses with courtesy and they, in turn, try to make him as comfortable as possible.

This morning he is confused. One of the nurses comes round asking if anybody wants a newspaper fetching from the shop.

'Bill?'

'Mmm. Yes?'

'Would you like a newspaper, love?'

'Mmm. Well, yes.'

'What would you like, Bill?'

'Mmm, well, potato please.'

'All right, love.'

I watch him now across the aisle. When his eyes are not closed in sleep he stares out as though he is peering towards the horizon, looking towards his next destination.

Out

Because the eating has been going well I am rewarded with the offer of a home visit. I immediately call Julie and ask her to collect me. I walk gingerly to the multi-storey car park. It's five minutes away but, on wasted muscles, it takes close on fifteen. The journey home is surreal, the daylight too vivid. Streets I have known for thirty years seem fresh and new. When we arrive back at the house I see that the front door has changed colour and only then do I remember I repainted it last summer. The dog approaches me tentatively and sniffs at the location of my stoma bag. She does not jump up in glee as she usually does. She senses something is wrong. I spend a relaxing day with my wife, son and daughter and sleep peacefully for an hour in bed, the first time I have slept on my side since I went into hospital. I know this place, this familiar smell, the towelly warmth of the bed sheets.

My daughter delivers me back to the ward at 7.30. I still need the proximity of the doctors and the reassurances of the nurses. I don't trust my body. I will be leaving permanently soon but the stoma bag is still collecting vile fluids and looks set to do so for some weeks to come. The nurse at the local GP surgery will deal with it when I get out of here permanently.

Shopping with Beelzebub

After finally being released and spending five days at home enjoying those things and people I'd for so long taken for granted I awoke on Saturday with a stabbing pain in my chest. I expected it to pass off. It didn't. I was glad I'd reserved full marks on the pain score because I could now award it. This was a full ten. I felt as though my ribcage had been clamped in a vice, the pressure had broken one of the ribs and the rib had punctured my lung. It was unbearable and unremitting. Julie delivered me to A&E a little before 8 a.m. They suspected a heart attack but an ECG showed that this was not the case. They took bloods and X-rays and found nothing. The conclusion was that it was muscular. I was sent home with painkillers.

Over the following five days the pain returned, each time more vicious. I visited A&E on two subsequent occasions and my GP once, each time being reassured it was either muscular or, perhaps, 'reflux', i.e., acid rising from my stomach and inflaming my oesophagus (this was the GP's assessment). Each time I was given stronger and stronger pain relief. When the pain returned for the fifth day I tried to reach the consultant who'd conducted my operation. One of his deputies told me to return to A&E and they'd get to the bottom of it. After a number of tests and scans it was discovered I now have gallstones and an inflamed gall bladder. It's the inflammation, plus the earlier damage that's causing the agony. I could have told them I had gallstones because I noticed a mention of it when I was reading my confidential surgical file (which somebody had left on my bed during my previous stay). Rapid weight loss is apparently a causal factor.

So after five days of freedom I'm back. Not in Beirut or the ward with the view of the marina. This is a ward on the west of the building, looking out over a car park. The inmates conform to the usual statistical breakdown. Two of the five are liver patients as a result of alcoholism. There is one tiny old man, roughly the size of a Borrower, and an often-changing patient in the bed closest to the door. Of the two liver patients the most interesting is the man to my left. He has an angry purple rash on both legs which at the ankles is hard and black – the skin crumbling like coal. Crohn's disease is suspected. He is a compelling presence, his voice like that of a night-time DJ on an offshore jazz station. He rarely stops talking but often the conversation is directed towards an imaginary congregation. Recent statements: 'You know I love you all very much. I'm very fond of you.' 'Egypt is dying, Egypt is dead,' 'I am the Count of Monte Cristo' and – my particular favourite from today, delivered when he was at the height of his pain – 'Beelzebub has visited and taken me shopping.'

Facing the DJ is another liver patient, Seasick Scott. He has a tumour on his hip. Cancer is suspected.

The tiny Borrower-sized old man is in great trouble. He can't swallow. His stomach is blocked. The Borrower's slippers are tiny with Power Rangers logos on them.

Pain

I've learned a lot about pain since I came in here and I now know I've been lucky to have avoided it for much of my life. I thought I knew what it was: the sharp sickly agony of a football to the testicles, nagging toothache, a paper cut, a knife cut to the finger, chronic stomach ache, a bad headache. That was the pain I knew: always manageable, recognisable, easily dealt with. But I now know pain comes in many more colours and intensities.

The nurses here have a chart displaying a series of cartoon facial expressions denoting differing degrees of pain. That way, when the agony is too intense for self-assessment, they can award it a score. On the ward it's easy to recognise which of the inmates is suffering. They are the ones who lie silent but not asleep, their breathing shallow, hands often clasped over the centre of the pain, staring straight down the barrel. It sounds obvious but I've learned that pain is easier to control when already under control, i.e., the regular application of painkillers is much more effective than using heavier doses when it's more intense. Paracetamol is a far more useful painkiller than one might have expected. Used in conjunction with morphine or codeine it's particularly good. However, both morphine and codeine dry up the system so constipation relief is best taken when using either.

The application of paracetamol-and-codeine has now rendered the agony of the inflamed gall bladder manage-able. Antibiotics will calm it down, with the hope that painkillers will no longer be required when the antibiotics have done their job. However, the consultant has just found a new way to inflict severe pain. On the ward round this morning I made the mistake of mentioning that the wound was tight and red. This prompted him to don a plastic apron and rubber gloves and stick his little finger as far as it would go into the wound (approximately 2 cm.

I later learn). As far as pain goes this was an eleven. I screamed an expletive. The attending medical students looked uncomfortable.

'Try and think about nice things,' the sister suggested. 'Breathe.'

I tried and failed on both counts as the consultant worked his finger around the rim of the wound, serrating a raw nerve I later learned had been exposed by the scalpel.

'I'm happy with that,' he announced, stripping off his gloves. 'Dry dress the wound and give him some Oramorph.'

Touching my arm comfortingly he apologised and went off to deal with the next patient.

Exit The Ghost

As I approached the end of the second stay in hospital The Ghost reappeared. It seemed too much of a coincidence and if I were writing a novel I would certainly not have reintroduced him at this point in the narrative. Nevertheless on my day of release I spotted him cleaning the windows of a Victorian pub close to the hospital. I had been told I was to be let out at lunchtime and having promised myself breakfast away from the ward I was walking gingerly to a local café to kill an hour or so (I'd been allowed out on day release for a while). Never having seen him out of pyjamas and dressing gown the figure in jeans and hoodie was unfamiliar. Only when he called, 'You all right, mate?' did the penny drop. I recrossed the road and we talked. I filled him in on my recent history and he told me he was still attached to his stoma bag but was going up to London for a second opinion on Friday. He was 'on the sick' and shouldn't have been working. We wished each other well.

As I crossed the road for the café he called, 'Remember! You didn't see me. You never saw me.'

Overheard on the ward an hour before departure

My bag is packed. I am dressed and am waiting for one last change of the wound dressing before I get a taxi home. I have just heard a consultant telling the Borrower that they now have the results of his tests and it's not good news. He has cancer and it is inoperable. The Borrower doesn't say anything. The consultant tells him he will have an oesophageal stent fitted which will help him eat and leaves him with some literature. When the curtains are pulled back and the consultant and his team leave I see that the tiny old man is poring over the leaflet he has been given. He looks towards me and smiles.

'All right?' I call. It's easy to pretend I haven't heard.

'Yes. They gave me a book,' he says proudly, holding it up, and for some reason the sight of it breaks my heart and for the first time in a couple of weeks I weep and weep and can't stop.

Intermission

Eight weeks in total were spent in hospital followed by six months at home recovering enough strength to get back to work. During this time the writing halted but I began to read again. Later, when I revisited one of Raymond Carver's short story collections, I came across this:

> You ought to write something in the journal
> during this period. How you feel and what you're
> thinking. You know, where your head is during
> this period of sickness. Remember, sickness is a
> message about your health and wellbeing. It's
> telling you things. Keep a record. You know what
> I mean? When you're well you can look back and
> see what the message was. You can read it later,
> after the fact.
> *Fever*

Carver's sage advice prompted me to type up the scrappy notes of the hospital journal – some completely illegible, some rambling, incoherent and insane – and send them off to the agent's. Because part of the journal chimed with the recent debate about increasing the unit price of alcohol in an attempt to reduce alcoholism the *Guardian*

163

Weekend published an extract. My publisher contacted me on the day the extract appeared suggesting it had put him off his morning sherry.

But the pre-hospital projects had all died and, along with them, a number of professional relationships. The divorce from PYD was brutal. He'd rewritten *An American Cockroach* a couple of times while I was out of commission and sent it out with what I considered to be ludicrous tranches of dialogue. I emailed him complaining vociferously when I finally got to see the latest draft. He argued (quite rightly) that he had needed to keep the project alive. He had, after all, optioned the story and had been informed I couldn't be reached. I argued (reasonably rightly) that I was unhappy putting my name to a script which bore little resemblance to what I'd delivered.

What morphine gives you in the short term it takes back with interest in the long term. Eight weeks of daily use plus a month weaning off it at home took its toll not so much on my physical but on my mental health. The withdrawal led not to sweats and cravings but to anger and hatred and paranoia.

It was not only the end of my relationship with PYD. Worse, I learned later that the film producer who had gone independent and worked with him had died, leaving a young family. I remember her mentioning at one of our meetings that she had a suspicious-looking mole on her leg. She was getting it investigated but claimed not to be worried about it.

Tasja oversaw the publication of the novel *Nimrod's Shadow* in April ('Agile, tricksy, doomy, smart and encompassing two storylines connected across two centuries, *Nimrod's Shadow* behaves suspiciously like a zinging, fifth-generation multi-vit' *Guardian*) but then left Portobello and went to live abroad with her family. The other TV and film projects, at the best of times fragile, all withered away.

But it didn't seem to matter. I was too busy trying to get well enough to live.

But over the following months the writing habit slowly returned in the form of a novel which began life as *The Keys* and went through a number of rewrites reflecting my changing moods and tastes and attitudes. It ignited when I read about an auction of the contents of Althorp, family seat of the Spencers. In the catalogue, alongside the carriages and artworks, was a set of garden keys. I loved the idea of somebody stumbling into an auction house one rainy afternoon, seeing the keys in the catalogue (which had been pressed into his hands as he walked in) and, on impulse, bidding for them. The novel began – a man with a set of keys searching for the locks they could open. No great leap of imagination to recognise that I was writing about my own journey and dressing it up as both a ghost story and a thriller. But the certainty with which I'd always approached novel writing had deserted me, and the early drafts reflected that. Deborah sent it out and got some nice rejections but quite rightly nobody wanted to publish. It just didn't work, and with my profile and recent sales record it had to work very well indeed. And then Deborah died suddenly leaving an unfillable gap in the lives of many. Her family and the publishing industry mourned her. The obituaries reflected on her brilliance and generosity and warmth. A publisher noted that when he heard Deborah's voice on the phone he sat up a little straighter.

Her clients were shared out around the agency or took the opportunity to jump ship. I was inherited by David, her former assistant, but not long after Deborah's death he too died far too young.

The novel was locked away but it was marinating somewhere in that place where unfinished stories are processed. A year, perhaps two, later I opened the computer file again and immediately knew what the novel needed. It was an ensemble piece, four siblings relating the same story from four conflicting viewpoints. Ivan (whose name I had borrowed from the old screenplay), the man who had bought the keys, was missing. In his quest to find the locks he may or may not have been involved in a terrible fire at a school. He may have been a victim or the perpetrator. The keys belonged to the school damaged by the fire, but what was he doing there? The novel came to life. I finished it and knew it worked in a way it hadn't before. Now I needed an agent prepared to take me on.

I was introduced to Tim by Dan, my former publisher. We met, had lunch, got on well and he said he'd be happy to represent me (I hadn't, at that point, revealed my recent history with those who'd worked with me – I thought I'd save that one). He asked me what I was working on. I told him that I had a novel on the stocks and about ten thousand words of diary pieces about a job I'd taken on as a casual in the local library. I'd applied for it after taking voluntary redundancy from the BBC on my fifty-fifth birthday. My health had never fully recovered and I knew that commuting 110 miles each day was doing me no good at all. A few months at home trying to write full time, something I'd always promised myself, taught me that I needed to get out of the house occasionally. Writing works best for me when there's pressure on the time you have to do it. And the imagination needs to be fed by some social interaction. Too many writers who write full time end up writing about writers writing (yes, I know, again the subject of this book). The casual job at the library served the purpose and, inevitably, I began keeping a journal. It began as a series of emails to myself after witnessing, or taking part in, bizarre and sometimes challenging incidents. All human life was there at the contemporary equivalent of the village pump.

Tim felt there was mileage in it and sold it. *Reading Allowed* was published in 2017 to more reviews and sales than the last three novels put together. The diary entries about the eccentric, troubled, sad and sometimes challenging customers of the city centre library and its community outposts were set against the effect of the cuts imposed by the local authorities which led to the cull of long-serving staff, and the closure of some of the outposts. Needless to say it was read with interest by those who worked in the service, but I should have anticipated that most of the readers borrowed rather than bought the book. Never mind. After ten years I was back in print. It mattered to me (if few others).

There was also a stage play – *The Final Test* – which toured the UK for three months in the summer of 2012 with Colin Baker in the lead. Although it didn't quite make it to the West End it was an interesting exercise to sit among a group of people and see and hear first-hand how they reacted to words I had written.

That was the last decade and the reason I decided to restart this journal was because finally, after years of on/off writing, I finished the novel which began life as *The Keys* back in October 2009. It's now called *Followers* and may be the last novel I write which is why I want to keep note of its progress as agent Tim reads it, responds to it and, hopefully, manages to secure a publisher for it. No mean feat. So here goes if you can bear it, once more round the carousel . . .

Part 3
Diary 2019 & 2020

There is no real ending. It's just the place
where you stop the story.

Frank Herbert

2019

9th January

Two weeks ago I emailed the final draft of *Followers* to Tim, who responded with a promise to read it a.s.a.p. A couple of days later I'd tinkered with it so much that I asked him to delete it with the promise I'd resend it when I'd stopped tinkering. It's now gone back to him and we've put a date in the diary in early February to have lunch and discuss it. He offered an earlier meeting but he's doing Dry January so wouldn't be drinking. As we don't meet that often I suggested we wait until he's wet again. I tried Dry January myself but lasted only three days. I have, however, cut down my alcohol consumption radically so am now doing neither wet nor dry, but slightly damp.

In ten years things have changed radically in the publishing and media industries. The me too. movement, a growing racial awareness and representation, and an increased sensitivity to gender inclusivity have changed the market. Surveys in the UK, USA and Canada taken in 2018 suggest that men account for only around 20 per cent of the fiction market. However, book clubs are dominated by women, as is library borrowing, as are creative writing groups.

Having worked in libraries for a few years now I can attest to the fact that the great majority of book borrowers are women. Or perhaps it only seems that way. To confirm or counter this theory I will take a non-scientific approach and count the number of male/female borrowers I encounter next Monday when I have a shift at the city centre library. I work as a 'casual library officer' which means I offer myself when available and if there are gaps in the rotas to be plugged, then I, and the other casuals, plug them. It might be illuminating also to take note of what they are borrowing. Perhaps this should have occurred to me earlier in the process of writing *Followers*, but I'm not sure it would, or should, have influenced the plot.

So this is the current state of the market into which Tim will be pitching the new novel. On the plus side *Reading Allowed* didn't do too badly and still seems to be getting interest on the Goodreads list. Reviews or ratings most days. It currently has an average appreciation of 3.79 (out of 5) and has had nearly four hundred ratings. The website is useful to take the temperature of what people like or dislike about your books. Instant feedback from a range of readers, another big change for writers. The one constant seems to be that what one reader likes, another hates. Further supporting evidence not to listen to opinions while writing.

22nd January

Prompted by rereading the 2007 writing journal I hunted around my old files for *The Store*, the unsold TV drama/comedy series which featured in so many producer/head-cold meetings. It stands up well although there are a few obvious problems with it which I've now rectified.

I spotted the name of the BBC executive I dealt with over the *Ivan* screenplay on the credits of a new ITV series last week so could try him with it.

In the meantime I've emailed Tim to ask if anybody in his agency deals with this kind of material and could have a look at it so I don't waste any more of my time with it. It seems to fit the zeitgeist more than it did a decade ago: an hour-long format, a mix of comedy and strangeness with a mystery at its heart. Netflix is currently dominating the market with hour-long episodes of unresolvable shaggy dog stories populated by eager, stupid, good-looking late teens. The premise of most of them is that something happens ten minutes into episode one – usually somebody going odd or a third of the world's population disappearing or committing suicide or something – and then, over the following four series, the conundrum continues to tease but is never resolved. The problem with this kind of drama is that, in the main, the writers don't have much clue as to what's happened to the bemused or disappeared characters so all they have to do is tease. The TV series *Lost* has a lot to answer for. The other popular genre is the 'nice middle-class family caught in a murky underworld situation'. *Breaking Bad* seemed to pave the way for this, and there have been many since. *Ozark* is the latest effort but it's a tried-and-tested format. *The Sopranos* and the other great TV dramas of the last fifty years, whatever package they're wrapped up in, are fundamentally about family dynamics. Libby, my ex-Radio-4-presenter chum, has, with her usual astute eye, pinned down a new TV genre: 'Bifold door dramas'. She's right – all of the 9 p.m. domestic TV series currently feature scenes set in a nice kitchen (extended, ceiling glass, exposed metal beams) with grey bifold doors leading out into the paved patio, then a short retaining wall, then the lawn.

Yesterday, during a shift at the library, I kept a tally of the numbers coming through the doors and, as predicted, around 80 per cent of those borrowing books were women. Also predictable was the fact that 100 per cent of the punters causing mayhem were men.

The council is currently conducting its annual review of services and library staff are being rota'd each day to canvass opinions. The questionnaire has four questions about the library itself (two of which are about how the service is accessed) and eight about the background of the person taking the survey: age, postcode, religious background, gender, whether they continue to present as the gender they were born, whether they have any particular needs, have served in the armed forces or are a carer. I'm sure this information will be of huge interest to the council and benefit to all the council taxpayers whose hard-earned cash is being spent on the survey. If a customer doesn't have access to the internet the staff member on survey duty has a tablet and offers them use of it. However, those who fall into that category are usually too old, poor, confused or disinterested to use it so ask the staff member to fill in the details for them: cue an awkward exchange in which a number of highly personal questions have to be asked. The over-seventies are generally bemused by the query over the fluidity of their gender identity whereas it's evident that the under-thirties wrestle with it on a daily, sometimes hourly, basis.

Staff not on rota duty are also encouraged to wander round and ask people reading or drinking coffee or chatting if they'd mind taking the survey. With this in mind I sidled up to a late-middle-aged man in a low comfy chair bent over the Brighton *Argus* and offered him the opportunity of having his voice heard. He was more than happy to do so, and spent the next forty minutes explaining his methadone habit, how the bailiffs have taken all his furniture, how all police in Brighton are 'c**ts', how the police up North are nicer, how the council has got access to his bank account and is regularly taking his money, 'but they've got the wrong f**king person, it's not me, see? So I tell them, you've got the wrong name, mate, I say this when I'm standing up in court. Read this, I say, is that my name? No it f**king is not so why am I here? You tell me that, mate, why am I here...?' And on, and on. The upside, he says, is that he's no longer living in a tent but has been provided with a flat and he can afford to eat, which is something. But the council still has access to his 'f**king bank account'.

Late in the day email back from Tim to say he'll ask the film/TV people for their advice and he's making good progress with *Followers* and enjoying it enormously, so some relief.

29th January

Awaiting the final verdict on the new novel I've been ruminating on the urge to continue to write. There's nobody clamouring for the new novel. It might not even find a publisher, but still the compulsion to spend hours, weeks, months of my life sitting – usually unhappily – at a laptop is there. Objectively I know it's a decent piece of work, and had I written it twenty years ago it would probably have been published, but, as I've mentioned, publishing has changed. I've been reading the novel that won the Costa prize in 2017, *Eleanor Oliphant is Completely Fine*. It's the first book for months I've not put aside before I finished it. As a novel it works. The writer is what Deborah would have described as 'the real thing'. It's her first published book (I doubt it's the first novel she has written). The protagonist is a complicated, well-drawn individual. The narrative is strong. I admire the fact that when she was interviewed (the book has sold massively across the world – the film rights have been bought by Reese Witherspoon) she refused to give anything away about her own life. Some of it is there on the page. None of the reader's business. *Publishing rule 17: Autobiography is fiction and vice versa.*

But, returning to the storytelling imperative, I realised a month or so ago that perhaps I inherited some of it from my mother. She's not a writer, but she has always read widely and has a habit of sometimes arriving at the point of a conversation via a circuitous route. The most recent example concerned my father's lost hearing aid. She told the story just before Christmas. My father hates his hearing aid and tends to take it out when in company, i.e., when he has most need for it. But his hearing aid went missing. They searched all over the house to no avail. Two days later they were eating soup (made by my father) for lunch. My mother encountered something solid in hers. She fished it out. Father's hearing aid. Rewind a couple of days to my father in the kitchen, making the soup. The phone rang in the lounge. My mother answered. It was for him. She took the phone into the kitchen. He removed his hearing aid to answer and, at that point, the hearing aid found its way into the saucepan. The coda of the story comes a couple of weeks later. My mother has been briefly hospitalised because of the flu. She is released but is weak; nevertheless she accompanies my father into town on the bus to pick up his new device. He collects it from Specsavers. She goes on ahead to the bus stop, falls and cuts open her head. People attend to her. She gives them her phone to call my father but, because he hasn't got his new hearing aid in, can't hear the phone ringing. He waits for her at the bus stop but she doesn't turn up. He sees a commotion at the other end of the queue. Somebody seems to be lying on the ground but, assuming trouble, he keeps his distance. It eventually dawns on him that the commotion might involve my mother. He goes to investigate and finds that, indeed, it is her. By taxi they return to the hospital.

The story is related to me by my mother, with some mirth and much detail.

5th February

Brighton doesn't tend to open to the public until mid-morning so the street community is more evident before those who have a roof over their heads get up. As I recorded in *Reading Allowed*, many street sleepers use the library for sanctuary, warmth and hygiene. I follow two of them on my way there for a long shift. Their light-coloured trousers are wet from the knees down – the dark grey of the material suggesting they have slept in a doorway which has sheltered their top half.

One is significantly taller than the other. The shorter one is better equipped with rucksack and walking boots and anorak. The taller one is wearing a thin T-shirt, and is carrying a Morrisons bag with a couple of cans of beer in it.

'Know why I got kicked out of my brother's?' he asks.

'No.'

'Ate one of his yoghurts.'

'No!'

'Straight up. He went f**king mental. I had to go. When I went back a few months later he said you didn't have to go for that. I said to him, you went f**king mental. And he said, "But you didn't have to go".'

'So you went back?'

'No f**king way.'

There's a pause. They begin to discuss abuse. Both have suffered it. The taller one says: 'Were you bait?'

The shorter one says, 'No it was more complicated than that . . . he died last year.'

'That make it better?'

'No.'

The exchange resonates with something I came across last night when I was going through some old box files of writing with a view to clearing them out. We're in the process of moving house and it's time I junked some of my archive. It's dominated the loft space of the last three houses we've lived in. Last year I offered it to The Keep, the local archive and resource centre which houses masses of local records and archive material. I've not been there yet but imagine it to look like the epic warehouse in the closing sequence of *Raiders of the Lost Ark*. My offer was greeted by enthusiasm by a senior archivist who said he'd forward it to his boss when he came back from leave. Unfortunately his enthusiasm wasn't shared on the grounds that they were being encouraged to reduce the amount of new material they accepted. He concluded: 'As manuscripts are borderline to our collecting policy and as the archive sounds fairly large I'm afraid we'll have to decline the offer.'

Nice rejection and the first from an archive – however, time now to get rid of it. I don't want the kids to be burdened by it when they clear out our final loft.

It wasn't until ten years after the unhappy writing experience at the hands of my English teacher at school that I wrote another story. By then I was working for the BBC. I remember sitting down in front of the fire one day in the basement kitchen of our small Brighton terraced house (warmth always features in these memories), getting out the typewriter my mother had donated to me and fumbling for the right words to use. It's called *The Foundry*. Rereading it today it clearly doesn't work, although the gothic atmosphere is strong. It belonged to a summer spent in north Derbyshire working for a company that was building, as the title suggested, a huge foundry. I was a 'bloody student', just there for the summer, so not the most welcome workmate to the hard men who had no choice but to make a living that way. The shifts were twelve hours long and, for a weakling, gruelling. But after a couple of weeks of humiliation, of growing muscle and the thick skin the school had deprived me of, I was accepted. It's one of the dozen or so jobs I have done which have filled the reservoir of experience I've drawn on in my writing: newspaper boy, supermarket shelf stacker, petrol-pump jockey, gardener, odd-job man and production-line worker in a cotton braid factory (a year-long job immediately post university, and one I thought I'd never escape), production-line worker in a cardboard manufacturing plant, bus conductor (undoubtedly the most enjoyable job of my life), electricity-meter reader, postman, delivery driver, finance clerk, sound engineer, radio producer, radio-programme editor, freelance journalist, odd-job assistant at Roedean School, university hall of residence cleaner (post-BBC the money was tight – see accounts for details), house painter, 'casual library officer' and, worst of all, pie-factory temp (scraping dry vomit-smelling residue from the aluminium trays that came out of the massive ovens – also post-BBC).

Unaware of how flawed *The Foundry* was I sent it off to the producer of *Morning Story* on BBC Radio 4. His name was Mitch Raper and he was a legendary figure, belonging to the pre-Birt BBC, an era in which producers had greater autonomy. Thirty years ago it was Mitch Raper alone who commissioned and produced a story every weekday on most weeks of the year. His production workload was massive. Alongside it he also took time to write back to those who'd offered stories he couldn't use, usually with a considered and gentle response (sadly I no longer have Mitch's kind rejections). He was an incredible man in terms of both productivity and generosity. I came to meet him when my BBC sound engineer's job led me to transferring from Bush House (World and Language services) to Broadcasting House (which housed the domestic national networks).

Mitch always wore battered, off-white tennis pumps. His feet were bad. He was lean, almost skeletal, with side-parted, untidy white hair, long at the collar, mischievous eyes. His casual jacket, worn over a white tie-less shirt, was loose, of a soft material and never buttoned. He carried his scripts along the corridors balanced precariously on a box of Kleenex tissues (along with troublesome feet he had problems with his sinuses). There was something of the Wild West about him: a hard-drinking, small-town quack. His 1995 obituary in the *Independent* noted: 'His methods were quite eccentric. A first encounter with him could be disconcerting. Arriving late and mumbling apologies this small, enthusiastic figure would linger over a cup of coffee, gossiping amusingly about Oxford or BBC intrigue before finally recording the story unrehearsed.'

Mitch didn't commission anything from me but turned down my stories graciously, always with an explanation and the encouragement and assurance that I was a capable writer and I should persist. His words began to undo some of the damage inflicted at school. Someone has to give you validation as a writer. I'm sure many other writers owe their careers to Mitch. I regret I never had the opportunity to thank him.

8th February

An email arrives from Public Lending Right (PLR), the body that allocates earnings to authors from library borrowings. When you've published a book and been allocated an ISBN you have the option of registering it with PLR which then monitors the number of times it has been issued by libraries. Each loan earns you 8.52 pence. This year the payment is a decent £409.05. *Reading Allowed* has been borrowed 4515 times. The others haven't found much favour, although *Nimrod's Shadow* went out around two hundred times, so not too bad. Must mention this to Tim when we meet.

I picked up a new collection of the essays of Jean-Paul Sartre on my last library shift (somebody had to). Interesting chapter on the American writer John Dos Passos. My mother gifted me his hefty USA trilogy when

I was a teenager and I started it but didn't get very far. I tried it again a couple of years ago with the same result so perhaps it's time to revisit it once again. Sartre uses Dos Passos as a springboard to discuss the experience of reading a novel.

> A novel is a mirror. Everyone says so. But what is it to *read* a novel? I believe that it is to jump into the mirror. Suddenly, you find yourself through the looking glass, among people and objects that seem familiar. But this is simply an appearance; in fact we have never seen them before. And the things in our world are now external in their turn and have become mere reflections. You close the book, climb back over the rim of the mirror, and re-enter *this* honest-to-goodness world, and you are back with furniture, gardens, and people who have nothing to say to you.
>
> *We Have Only This Life to Live:*
> *The Selected Essays of Jean-Paul Sartre 1939–1975*

I love that glimpse into Sartre's worldview: ' . . . furniture, gardens, and people who have nothing to say to you'. Hopefully not the case when I meet up with Tim later for lunch in Covent Garden.

Balthazar is a large-scale French restaurant with the atmosphere of a small, intimate place. The mâitre d' greets Tim with enthusiasm and seems genuinely pleased to see him. It's a rare talent and one of the few a good mâitre d' needs. It's over a year since we last met and we catch up on the news but I'm on edge, aware that this is the verdict meeting on *Followers*. It's many years since I last delivered a novel and I'm taken back to those lunches with Deborah. She must have hosted hundreds of them and was always cautious when it came to promises. Wherever we met in North London Deborah would always arrive by car, always a little late, always a little flustered, apologetic that she had lost track of the time, couldn't find a parking space, had been caught on the phone by a publisher on her way out. She'd be brimming with news, and always a little reluctant to shift from gossip to a discussion of the work in progress.

Thankfully, not long into the first glass, but before we order, Tim broaches the subject. He smiles. He knows I'm waiting. He loved it, he says. Normally he hates multi-voiced narratives, but this one he feels works because the voices are differentiated. I hate multi-voiced novels too, I admit, but it couldn't be helped with this one. You just have to go with what the characters are demanding of you. We briefly discuss the structure and the content. He cautions that it's incredibly hard at the moment with literary fiction, but says that potentially this could find a wide readership if it's handled well. We need to get it to the right publisher with plans and enthusiasm. He has a few ideas but he wants a senior editorial guru at the agency to read it first and offer his thoughts. He's concerned that we make it as watertight as possible before he sends it out. The main issue is how we flag it up: mystery, ghost story, thriller? It is all of these things. He suggests I write a blurb to help him get a handle on how I see it. The library journal *Reading Allowed* was sold on the strength of a lengthy pitch document. Gone are the days of a few words scrawled on the back of a fag packet and handed over after a liquid lunch in Soho.

We'll meet again in a month or so to talk about what needs to be done editorially but he wants to get it out soon. Finally he asks about my health. Since the hospital stay recorded in Part 2 there has been another, this one longer, for bowel cancer. Again the operation went wrong, again I was an unwilling guest of 'Digestive Diseases' for a protracted period. You don't realise what a privilege good health is until it's withdrawn from you. Nevertheless I assure him that all is OK for now.

On the way home I ruminate on how I would have felt if he hadn't liked the book. Artists need a thick skin. Being 'rejected' or knocked back is part of the process of defining your voice. A writer therefore needs to be able to trust the instincts of his agent or those whose opinions he trusts because he could be wrong, misguided, deluded in his belief that what he has to say is being delivered accurately. Once that voice is defined the agent has another – almost more important – role to play in judging whether he still has relevance and will therefore find a publisher. I've always been out of step with whatever was selling; not quite showily literary enough for the prizes nor commercial enough for the mass market, which has always made my agent's job difficult. But I've been privileged to have had people who believed enough in what I had to say to ensure it could be heard by others.

But what if the new novel had been complete rubbish? I ask this of Tim as we part and he suggests it would have been a much shorter lunch: 'A glass of tap water and piss off home.'

28th April

Another month of writing *Followers* and today is the

meeting with agent Tim and Tim Two (editorial guru at the agency). They've now had the latest version and we're going to spend some time grinding down the rough edges. On the way to the station a street sleeper is standing at attention with four bottles of Becks lined up at his feet. One is empty. He's not looking for change but repeats a single statement again and again across the empty street: 'You startled my aunt, you startled my aunt, you startled my aunt...'

I'm due to meet Tim at the West End office of the agency where he works. It's a more corporate set-up than Deborah's, occupying a high floor of a modern office block close to Tottenham Court Road. The reception alerts you to the fact you've entered a place where literary endeavours are conducted: floor-to-ceiling shelves of hardback books, some of them quite old, signalling that although the agency is in a modern building it's been around much longer than its location might imply. Once it was owned and run by literary types, now corporate bankers. Beyond the reception and the chatty receptionist you can see the open-plan acres, the air of determined and almost silent activity, the youngish staff in casual media dress speaking quietly on phones or surveying computer screens, oat-milk lattes evident. In the distance are a few glass-fronted pods where people can plot undisturbed.

Tim collects me from reception and takes me to his pod (he's quite senior so is one of the few allowed partition walls for privacy). There we're joined by Tim Two who I now realise I met years ago at a party at my then agent's – a wonderful novelist just a little older than I whose parallel life has been spent in publishing. Tim Two is grateful that he's just sold his latest novel to Bloomsbury. It might, he says, be the last one he writes. Both have reread the manuscript, made notes, and we set to discussing them. Both suggest we could use the thriller element of the plot more effectively (I see immediately that I've used the collective 'we' – the book is now in shared ownership). The other issue is the character of a young female: too brazen and not nuanced enough when introduced. There are perhaps a dozen suggested tweaks, all of which will be noted in a marked-up manuscript which he'll email to me.

A novel is not finished when the author's final draft is delivered to the agent. Meetings such as these are an integral part of the process because for the first time the dialogue you had with yourself is being tested for its truth against the way others process the world. Publication will, if you're lucky, be the end point, but the editorial process is an important part of the conversation you have been having with yourself. Somebody else has entered your cosy room and joined in. Successful agents and publishers are teachers and most successful novelists are always pupils, albeit sometimes reluctant ones. *Publishing rule 18: Writing is rewriting. Publishing rule 19: The age of a publisher or agent has less to do with his or her effectiveness than their wisdom.*

29th April

I've now begun what I think will be the final rewrite of the novel. I'm still not bored with it. As I've changed, grown older, been stripped of the certainty of good health, jettisoned 'BBC radio producer' as part of my identity, become a grandfather twice over, the storyteller has changed and so has the story he is telling. I now know what the keys in the novel are for, and which doors they can and, as importantly, cannot open. I'm not sure how these changes are reflected in my writing. I know I trust my instincts more when it comes to examining and representing how people relate to each other but I'm not sure whether I'm a better or worse writer than I was when I began. You learn a few new tricks and maybe forget some of the old ones. The one constant is to maintain a freshness of vision when you're rewriting the work in progress. When the novel is published, that vision has gone which is why I rarely reread my books in print. When I try I see only their shortcomings and often don't have much sympathy or love for the writer. I can see what he was up to.

Since I left the BBC I've begun to paint. About five years ago for Christmas Julie bought me two art lessons with a friend, a brilliant watercolour artist, Kate Osborne. I hadn't painted since O-level art but always intended that one day I would. Those two lessons opened up a new way of storytelling. I loved it and soon discovered that it was not so dissimilar to writing in that you began by defining the lights and darks, the colour tones, the overall shape, and then refine, refine and refine until you had got somewhere close to the impact you set out to achieve. Yes, you always fall short, but eventually you reach the point where you stop balling up sheets of soggy paper and hurling them in the bin. I proudly framed my first relatively successful line-and-wash painting: *Brighton's Theatre Royal*. It hangs on the wall in the small basement room in which I paint.

At school 'Art' was never really taught in the same way as other subjects. We learned no techniques but were just encouraged to express ourselves ('You like colour, don't you?' was one of the more memorable steers from the art teacher). The two lessons with Kate confirmed that I had a facility for the medium which perhaps lay in my family's history. Both my grandfather and great-uncle earned their living as painters. When I began with Kate I learned that a bead of watercolour paint at the bottom of a descending curtain (the paper would be taped to a board and angled at around 45 degrees) would always allow itself to be diverted and redirected. It would populate only the moist area of the paper and refuse to colonise the dry. So long as the paint was wet it was malleable.

So it is with stories. The paint of the current novel is still wet. There's also a new title. *Followers* wasn't right. Too many social media associations. The first one, *Into the Silent Land*, was discarded a few months back. The new title is *Like the Living*. It comes from a Colette quote (she's a significant force in the narrative) and is intended to serve both as an injunction and observation. We'll see if it sticks.

21st May

Novels are, as I've mentioned before, written largely by the unconscious mind and merely transcribed by the novelist. But when a narrative is being processed the mind calls in other elements of autobiography, testing to see how they can be of use. Sometimes at night when you awaken you catch your mind at it. These are the threads that were tied last night in the waking hour between 2 and 3 a.m.:

1. Twenty-five or so years ago I met Jed Mercurio at a Jonathan Cape party. Cape had just published his first novel, *Bodies*. We talked vaguely about a collaboration. He was working on some projects for television. We got on fine but have never met since.

2. Last night Julie and I watched the final episode in series one of *Bodies* which the BBC have re-released following Jed's huge success with *Line of Duty* and *Bodyguard*. *Bodies* premiered on BBC Three in 2004, ran for two series and culminated in a feature-length finale, earning criticism from the government for its portrayal of the target-driven NHS. In a recent interview Jed, who worked as a hospital medic, acknowledged that *Bodies* is the project he's most proud of. For me, it remains the best thing he's done.

3. The name of the director on two episodes of *Bodies* is one I recognise. It's somebody I came across at the BBC when I jumped ship from 'local radio accounts', where I was employed briefly, post-university, as an inept finance clerk. The department was run by an Arthur Daley character who enjoyed liquid lunches and slept most afternoons, feet up on the desk, aftershave getting stale, tie loose. On my first day I spotted an advert in the BBC internal paper (*Ariel*) for studio managers (BBC Radio's sound engineers – I'd failed the external board for the traineeship after leaving university) and applied. After walking back to Cavendish Square from Broadcasting House where I'd found my personnel officer and lodged the application I was called in and loudly carpeted – quite rightly. My irate new boss suggested I give it a few months before attempting to escape his empire. The call from personnel had interrupted his nap. A year later I reapplied to become an SM and, that time, was accepted. One of the clerks who allocated the shifts for the sound engineers was the man who directed

two episodes of *Bodies*. Like me, he escaped clerkdom. Ultimately he became the all-powerful Head of Drama for the BBC. Mobility was possible then.

4. Last week I was listening to *Ed Reardon's Week* on Radio 4. I'm sure most listeners regard it as satire. For me it's autobiography. Ed, for those who haven't encountered him, is a struggling freelance writer. Early success sees him peaking with penning an episode of the TV drama series *Tenko*. Thirty years on he's divorced, penurious, living in a shed with his cat, Elgar, and grubbing a living with freelance gigs (*Kevin Pietersen's Barbecue Bible* etc.) found for him by his agent Ping. In last week's episode, Ed calls up the BBC *Writer's Room* to try and get taken on, suggesting that he's actually Ed Mercurio, Jed's brother. It fails to get him the gig. Fay, my former film agent, approached the *Writer's Room* for me twenty-odd years back but I was turned down for a reason I can't remember (so no hack work on *Doctors*, *Holby* or *'Stenders* on my CV).

5. *Bodies* highlights the constraints put on treatment by targets in the NHS. The consultants' care for their patients is outweighed by their concern for their treatment, mortality and morbidity rates. Next week I have a follow-up appointment with the consultant who conducted the operation I had for bowel cancer. As in my previous stomach operation (recorded in part two) the bowel tore post-op and again I ended up in 'Digestive Diseases' for eleven weeks. At one point I was given a brutal '46 per cent chance of survival' by my consultant, and was reminded regularly by him that 'You might not make it,' and 'We need to discuss whether you should

sign a DNR [do not resuscitate] form.' I think he missed the bedside-manner lecture at med. school. It wasn't much fun. After my eventual release Julie and I visited him for a follow-up. When we walked into his office he was working at his PC. He looked up, turned the screen towards us and said, 'I've been updating my figures. Here . . .' He pointed a long surgeon's finger towards the bottom line which showed the number of operations he'd performed in which the bowel had subsequently torn. 'Less than 3 per cent,' he explained. I apologised for messing up his figures. If I ever meet Jed again I'll mention this to him.

6th November

Dealing with the NHS has become an all-encompassing new hobby and explains the latest hiatus. A routine cancer follow-up scan picked up a couple of potential areas of concern. This was followed by another which seemed to confirm cancer in the left lung and a 'highly suspicious pre-sacral mass', i.e., a possible recurrence of the initial cancer. I was handed over to 'Lungs' which resulted in a booking in London for an operation in which a robot will remove the upper half of the top globe of my left lung, hopefully with a human in attendance. Apparently you can get by without it. The mass might be benign but it's too deep to get a needle in for a biopsy. It's also sitting against the aorta and if that gets punctured then it's *Goodnight Vienna*. Anyway, that's next Thursday up at Guy's.

There's a convention among writers and media folk that, should they fall seriously ill, they will write about it or make TV documentaries about it. It's sold as 'helping people in the same condition'. What it is in truth is 'look at my pain'. Suffering in silence is not an option for writers and rarely a day goes by on TV without one of the presenters revealing his or her brave battle with cancer. The truth is that, with cancer, the battle is being fought on your behalf primarily by others, the sufferer merely the battleground. Clearly I've fallen victim to this syndrome myself. Anyway, operation next week then, presumably, recovery at home if it all goes well. I must be owed at least one operation that goes without a hitch. Definitely no journal this time.

After lunch today, on the street, I bumped into a friend who's also been suffering with cancer for a few years. He'd just had a letter from the hospital telling him he has to have a kidney out. Nothing wrong with it but the cancer lies behind it so they need access. I told him about the lung removal which, along with the two lengths of bowel, my gall bladder, appendix, tonsils, adenoids and other bits and pieces the NHS has nicked has severely depleted the number of internal organs I now own. We discussed the possibility of pooling those we have to make up a fully functioning human being. The issue would be whose head is used. We agreed to discuss it further.

There has been a recent flurry of interest in *Reading Allowed*. A friend texted Julie to tell her it was being discussed on Radio 4's *A Good Read*. Didn't have a clue they were doing it, but it went down well with Stewart Lee, Dave Haslam and the presenter Harriett Gilbert, who chose it. Gratifyingly they picked up on the main issue I hoped the book would raise – the vital societal importance of libraries. The exposure briefly rocketed the book up the Amazon chart to 260.

Spoke to Tim yesterday who suggests glimmers of interest here and there in *Like the Living* and a number of nice rejections. Selling fiction is more political nowadays. The editors have less autonomy. There's less money around to splash out. Marketing has always been involved in purchasing decisions but now I sense more so. The conglomerates are business oriented and less likely to employ people who'll take a punt on something unusual (though writers continue to assume they're fundamentally charitable institutions set up to support them).

Interesting moment in the library last week when I was in there for a short shift. I can only manage 8.30 a.m.–5 p.m. nowadays. Since the recent health issues the 8.30 a.m.–7 p.m. is too gruelling. A street sleeper came in damp and cold and asked for a book recommendation – something local. I suggested *The Gorse Trilogy*, Patrick Hamilton's wonderful collection about a Brighton con artist (although it does decline as the trilogy progresses and his drinking intensifies). I found it on the shelf for him and issued it but it wouldn't fit in his pocket so he returned it and went off in search of a smaller book. *Publishing rule 20: Lesson for writers there – write shorter books if you want a readership among the street community.*

Health however is dominating thoughts. Trev, the security man at the library, wishes me well as I leave at the end of my final shift. He's an NHS regular and has a tattoo done each time they remove another bit of his body. Apparently he looks like Ray Bradbury's *Illustrated Man*.

22nd November

I seem to have dodged a bullet. The operation went well and less than forty-eight hours after having the top left globe of my lung out I was back on the train to Brighton with Julie feeling better than I expected. After experiencing the NHS at its worst a couple of years back, I've now enjoyed them operating at their best (literally). I shared a ward with nine others and, therefore, the details of their lives. The man opposite Skyped his 'missus' each night. I tried not to listen, but it was conducted at such a volume it was impossible not to. 'The house is so f**king empty without you, babe,' is something that remains in my mind. To my right was a suave late-middle-aged man in nice pyjamas who cast himself as the hero of his own misfortune. He rang as many people as he could during the day, bravely reporting the minutiae of his operation. 'Look at my pain' is of course not solely the preserve of the media classes.

Back home to receive an email from the TV person at the agent's who had read the first episode of *The Store*. He liked it but said he'd never sell it. I have no track record so nobody will chance it. Despite the proliferation of TV outlets, he says it's becoming harder to sell to TV without a name or a track record. He suggests I write it as a novel because it would then be more saleable. TV companies are more likely to take a chance on a first-time novelist as a scriptwriter. I can tell, I said, given the quality of the UK's TV drama. I suggest to him that if we could sell the one that's currently doing the rounds I might try *The Store* next.

Several months now and no bites, although apparently things are stirring and a pre-op email from Tim suggests he 'hopes to have some rousing news soon'. We'll see.

2020

18th January

The news on *Like the Living* is not yet rousing. Nearly eight months now and the bidding frenzy has yet to ignite. Only a matter of time, I'm sure.

The painting side of my life has, however, flared into life. I've just sold a big canvas at a decent gallery in Lewes who took me on as a 'visiting artist' alongside the proper painters they represent. After learning the rudiments of watercolour painting from Kate I experimented with acrylics and then oils which I found the most conducive to work with. Oils are demanding in a different way from watercolours. They do what's asked of them in that you can put them onto a surface with a brush or a knife or your fingers and they don't encroach on what's around them – but they are stubborn. Mess them around too much and they'll get very muddy. But handle them with care and they'll repay you with rich, deep images which seem to reach beyond the canvas. It takes a lifetime to master the many techniques you can use and I'm a latecomer to the medium, but I recognise that I'm looking for a similar voice to the one I use in the writing. I don't want the medium to draw attention to itself. I strive to render an image accurately and to provoke some sense of recognition, but also surprise. The painters I've grown to revere (Manet, Hopper, Sickert, Ravilious, Cézanne and many others) all do that. They take possession of a place in time and hand it back to you redefined: 'Here is how I see it, but now you do some work and bring your own feelings to it.' Again, not that dissimilar to writing. A good novelist treats the reader with respect and understands that although he or she may be beginning the conversation the reader is a contributor to it and has to be left that space to contribute.

One thing that has struck me, however, is that I have absolutely no visual memory. By that I mean that when I write I can see clearly the scene and the characters I'm writing about. When I paint I need the image in front of me – usually a photograph I've taken. Without that image I'm lost.

The gallery in Lewes is, however, now changing hands so I've been trying to find local representation. After firing off a few emails to Brighton galleries last year to stony silence I tried one more just before Christmas. I have seven or eight paintings up in the local café/gallery based on some of the first Kodachrome photographs taken by the Farm Security Administration photographers in the States in the thirties and forties. Their job was to chronicle the life of the rural poor, a New Deal initiative. The photos are as evocative as Edward Hopper's paintings. My favourite is a 100 x 150 cm. oil painting based on a photograph taken by John Vachon of a steam locomotive in the snow. I sent an image to a gallery close to the Town Hall in Brighton. They responded an hour later and took me on. Like most galleries they take 50 per cent for their trouble but they have a good reputation and it means at least a few of the canvases can be taken out of the clutter in the basement 'art room' and hung on a wall.

Painting, as I've mentioned, is in the genes. From the age of fourteen until he retired fifty years later my paternal grandfather worked for British Railways painting the signage on the stations and graduating to painting the crests on locomotives and carriages. His brother, my great-uncle Chris, after whom I was named, was a talented amateur painter and a professional stage scenery artist.

Chris served in the Royal Army Medical Corps in the Great War. Something happened to him in France – he hinted at it without revealing exactly what – but it led to him being wounded and hanging upside down by his leg in a trench for several hours. After the war he became a theatrical stage manager and, for a few years, worked in northern theatres, also writing and producing musicals and pantomimes. His sanctuary was a wooden hut on a remote farm in Alderley Edge. At Christmas he was responsible for looking after the monkeys which appeared in the pantomimes and he'd take them to the hut where (my father recalls) they clambered along the washing line strung across the ceiling and caused mayhem by showering the people below with their droppings.

Chris left stage management and set up his own theatrical scenery suppliers. My father remembers visiting his huge Manchester warehouse as a child. Chris, shirt-sleeved, would be high up on a platform with a cigarette in one hand and a huge paintbrush in the other, several silver cans of paint at his feet as he worked on the scenery cloths – 40 feet (or more) square. The cloths were painted from the top down, the platform lowered by a rope as the image developed. When a fire cost him his warehouse and his company he moved to Fitups, which provided scenery for the fledgling TV industry in Manchester.

His company was also responsible for the panoramic murals used by the RAF to train pilots on the early flight simulators ('link trainers') during the Second World War. One of my earliest memories is being carried on my father's shoulders across railway tracks and taken into a vast ware-house where the huge scenery flats were stored. I can't have been more than one year old but the memory is vivid, as is that of sitting beside my great-uncle on the leather bench seat of his old Jaguar, being driven at high speed up the then empty M1 motorway. Chris had his arms crossed, so was not even steering the car, and he was smiling. He was considered a 'character', but his war experiences always haunted him. He was married to a long-suffering woman we called Auntie Dorothy. Chris would go out for fish and chips and disappear for days. He died when I was very young but my memories of him are some of the most vivid from my childhood, and one of my most treasured posses-sions is a landscape he painted in oils.

I didn't realise how good he was until I started painting myself. I also have some of his pantomime scripts and a piece of his personal writing paper. Across the top, proudly declared – CHRIS PALING. Writer, director, producer – and his Manchester telephone number.

From my grandfather Alf I inherited a set of signwriter's paintbrushes, from my great-uncle Chris a love of land-scapes and some facility for writing. I feel them both at my shoulder when I paint.

I'm lucky in that my work has begun to sell. The canvas sold in Lewes went for half what I got for my last novel. There's no question that the technique and imperative is basically the same: choose an image – edit it to fit, render it as accurately as you can but make it speak with your voice, refine it until it tells the story you want it to tell. Try to make the viewer feel something of the way you did the first time you saw the image.

Yes – just try to make them feel.

The library continues to furnish stories each day, though I'm resisting writing a follow-up to *Reading Allowed*. One of the recent books I returned for a customer was *The Selfish Giant* by Kazuo Ishiguro. I've mentioned it before but Ish and I shared an agent, Deborah. Ish was one of her favourites and, of course, one of her superstars. The dedication is, simply, 'Deborah Rogers', followed by the year of her birth and that of her death.

24th January

Brief phone conversation with Tim on the prospects for *Like the Living*. No bites, but he's seeing Andreas in two weeks to discuss projects. An uncanny echo of 2008 when Deborah was awaiting a response to *Nimrod*. We discuss sending it out under a *nom de plume*. I'd be happy with that. I'm not proud – I'm a literary stealth bomber, after all.

The newspapers today are reporting an unusual use for cheese:

> A cheese slice bookmark has given librarians and thousands of social media users a Gouda laugh.

A tweet about the slice, found at the University of Liverpool library, has been shared more than twenty thousand times.

Associate director Alex Widdeson said the 'disconcertingly warm and liquid' slice was discovered 'somewhere between American history and geography'.

She said while library users were '"Brie" to eat cold food . . . we prefer them not to use snacks as bookmarks.'

8th February

An email from Tim to say he's seeing Andreas for lunch this coming week and will be discussing *Like the Living* and this journal. I decided to send an extract of it to him a couple of months ago to see if it had any potential. Like the library journal it wasn't written with a view to publication but it struck me that there might be something in it. I then went back through it, fearing that I might have revealed more of myself than I intended to, and was perhaps too disparaging of the literary world. Too late now.

The other development on the writing front came when I googled my play, *The Final Test*, yesterday. After its three-month theatrical tour with 'The sixth Doctor Who, Colin Baker' in the lead (a very impressive and undersung comic actor), the play was published and is now occasionally picked up by an amateur group. You, as writer, are never alerted to this. Why should you be? But occasional web surfing reveals a nice surprise. This time I learn it's to be performed in New South Wales for ten nights over a month-long period. I email the director to wish them all luck and ask for photos from the production.

I fell under the spell of theatre when I was a teenager. My father was an enthusiastic member of a local amateur drama group. They put on two plays each year in the church hall and got decent audiences: ninety or a hundred each night. After a brief apprenticeship I was given the responsibility for the stage lighting. For three nights, plus a Sunday afternoon dress rehearsal, I'd sit in a hot lighting booth high above the auditorium and follow the cues in the script, fading lights up and down as required. For someone who hated being under the spotlight it was perfect. I had control of it and could participate without being seen.

It was the same a decade later when I became a radio producer. A producer's job is to provide whatever is needed by those whose ego is big enough to warrant them sitting at a microphone to entertain or inform the nation. I had no interest in addressing the microphone myself, but knew what those who had needed to do it well.

Watching those well-made three-act plays from the lighting gallery – *Blithe Spirit*, *Boeing Boeing*, *Gaslight*, *Dangerous Corner*, a few Alan Ayckbourns and many others – I began to see how they were shaped, and when I tried writing them myself undoubtedly borrowed from what I'd seen. I wrote the stage play *The Final Test* shortly before I left the BBC. When the idea came to me I knew it wouldn't suit a novel. A man, asleep in a deckchair in his garden, cricket commentary on the radio, the newspaper covering his face gently rising and falling with each breath; the arrival of a removal man in a brown coat announcing to the sleeping man they were packed and ready to go. It was a stage play: a clearly defined single space, a timeframe that would suit three acts, a dilemma that could be explored and perhaps resolved. It fitted the requirements for the 'two-hour traffic' demanded by drama. Ideas, when they arrive, tend to be attached to a genre without that attachment ever being questioned and when an idea is transplanted from one genre to another (the *Whales* film, for example) it rarely works.

Libby read the finished play and passed it on to a producer she knew. He liked it and passed it on to another – one of the few still touring original plays. And so I found myself one afternoon sitting round a table in the closed bar of a theatre in Worthing with a director, six actors and a stage manager with a stopwatch. Forty-odd years since I'd last sat in that lighting gallery I was watching professional actors reading my words out loud – and laughing at the right places, and becoming the characters I'd written. And they were nervous of me. I could see it. Somehow my opinion of their performance mattered to them.

The play toured for three months. Julie and I saw it in Cambridge and Bournemouth and Derby. Like most plays it failed to make money, but the experience of sitting among an audience responding to what I'd written was illuminating. Novelists rarely get that visceral reaction to their words. Playwrights live on it. It's addictive.

I wrote another play: *Dr Winstanley's Miracle Cure*, a tight three-handed thriller, which I think is better than the first but it has yet to be performed. But again, as so often in the past, I'm grateful that somebody has taken a chance on something I've written and brought it to life.

13th February

Fact is, indeed, occasionally stranger than fiction. Email from Tim yesterday at around 4.55 p.m., following his lunch with publisher Andreas. I assume he arrived back from lunch earlier, but could be wrong. In fact I hope I am wrong, much preferring to be represented by somebody who still enjoys a decent lunch. Few people drink nowadays at lunchtime.

I'm assuming he was punting a number of projects to Andreas but, strangely, the thing that ignited his interest was mention of this journal. This, obviously, steers it into uncharted territory and all new entries will be written with the understanding that they might end up being published by the publisher who is being written about, and being sold by the agent who also features in it. I suppose this is what is considered to be 'meta'. I've never quite understood the term but it seems to apply now. So Tim's sending the journal to Andreas, and I have to shut up for a while because I'm now concerned that anything I do write might influence the journal's prospects. But I should add that Tim carefully avoided any discussion of the novel, so clearly Andreas has not snapped it up. It would, as I suggested to Andreas in an email this morning, make a strong pairing with this journal should he decide to publish it. Or maybe not. As I said, uncharted territory.

On the upside, I learn that two friends have both just sold their books. One is a retired hospital consultant, who I met when he treated Julie and we became friends. His memoir is terrific and a small publisher has made an offer. The other is friend Duncan who's been commissioned to do a book of commissioned essays on walking. He's cornered the market on walking anthologies.

The play, *The Final Test*, opens tomorrow in New South Wales. The director sent me a photo of the set which is astonishingly good – better, in fact, than the professional set used in the UK tour. It promises well.

14th February

I wake to find a message on my website which I vainly set up to market my paintings (www.chrispaling.com). I don't get many, despite the contact form. In fact, I've had only five messages in a couple of years, which included a couple from Julie's friend who designed the site, testing the link. So only three. Actually one was from me checking that the link was still working, so just two, one of which was from a man who wanted to help me with my marketing. Today's is from one of the readers who recommended my play, *The Final Test*, be performed by Woy Woy Little Theatre in NSW Australia. It's full of praise for the production and the response to it. She reports that 'There was much laughter and we were also moved by the true-to-life situations.'

It's heartening, and rare, to get such an affirmation. Writers often claim not to need it. But they do. I email back my gratitude.

Today will be devoted, in part, to painting. I've decided to do a series of 90 x 90 cm. paintings of the local shops. North Laine, to which we've now returned after moving further and further out of the city over the years, is full of independent traders. Being part of a community has become increasingly important since I gave up commuting and began to take proper root in Brighton.

I've also become more curious about the lives of artists (more so than the lives of writers), and came across this quote the other day when I was reading about Picasso; he suggests:

> We all know that Art is not truth. Art is a lie that makes us realise truth, at least the truth that is given us to

understand. The artist must know the manner whereby
to convince others of the truthfulness of his lies.

Art – the lie that tells the truth. A novel, after all, is also
just an extended lie. There was no 'Once upon a time'. It
never happened, so why, over the centuries, have people
willingly allowed themselves to be taken in by these lies?
Because, of course, of the truth behind them.

As true in a painting as in a novel or a play.

20th February

Yesterday we met our daughter and two grandchildren
at Nymans, a National Trust property north of Brighton.
The weather was damp, but we wanted to see the
Quentin Blake exhibition there. Walking round the
gardens I trailed Julie and daughter Sarah (pushing the
buggy) and wondered, as I always do, how the child we
seemed to have had yesterday is now approaching forty
and has two children of her own. I was walking hand-
in-hand with grandson Luca (four), who had paused to
straighten a daffodil which had been blown to an angle
of 45 degrees by Storm Dennis. He managed to rest it
against a colleague for support. We pressed on. 'Did you
know,' he said, 'that a bell rings every time a flower
comes out?'

'Where?'

'In the flower.'

'I didn't know that.'

What I particularly liked about the Quentin Blake
exhibition was the case displaying a few of his dip pens
and doodlings and the scruffy biro page on which he
mapped out his layouts. The colours of the prints are

vivid: deep, rich watercolours which seem casual but are obviously not.

I'm reading one of Blake's contemporaries, Raymond Briggs, at the moment. His last book, I'm sure. We pass his house sometimes when we're out and about beyond the Downs on the Vespa. At the end of his lane is a signpost which bears resemblance to the one in *The Snowman*. His new book contains curmudgeonly reflections on his approaching demise. He's always been a grump. Sometimes his work is described as 'sad', but it's better viewed as melancholic which is quite a different thing even though it perhaps comes from the same source. It's deep-rooted in him. The drawings in *Time for Lights Out* are pencil, slightly undefined, the dialogue above them hard to read, like listening to an old man's voice which is fading. It's eminently quotable. I particularly liked his definition of a business meeting. Not so far from that of the producer/head-cold format.

> A business lunch meant going somewhere you
> would rather not go to meet people you would
> rather not meet to eat food and drink drink you
> will later regret to make plans that more often
> than not come to naught and spend money that
> could better be spent.
>
> *Time for Lights Out* Raymond Briggs

The house phone rings at about 10.30 a.m. and I ignore it. Nobody that we want to speak to uses it. I then get an email from publisher Andreas to tell me he's trying to reach me and will I call him. This immediately ignites my interest. *Publishing rule 21: When publishers call you, you stand a decent chance of selling something to them. If you have to call them, chances are negligible.* I try him. He's busy doing an email, will I call him back in five? I do. He says he's going to find a pod so he can talk to me. Andreas works in an open-plan office which, as anybody who works in one will attest, makes it impossible to do any work requiring any degree of confidentiality or potential embarrassment. When he's found an unoccupied pod, Andreas tells me he's read the journal, passed it on to his colleague and she wants to take it to the acquisitions meeting next week. Can I write a five-hundred-word pitch? I tell him that I will. I take the chance to ask Andreas about his views of the novel. He says that he liked it, but wouldn't want to publish it and 'sell about three hundred copies'. He feels it would have a greater chance of being sold and published if this journal is commissioned.

Returning to the issue of open-plan offices, I spent much of my BBC life in Broadcasting House, 'B. H.', or 'Old Broadcasting House' as it's labelled now that they've nailed a new bit on the side, 'new Broadcasting House' (lower case 'n' apparently), which sits there like a ghastly doppelganger and cost around a billion quid. Fiona et al. present the news from the new bit. When I started at the BBC, B. H., designed by George Val Myer in the 1920s, had hundreds of small offices around the exterior of the building, with the studios isolated from the street noise (but not tube rumble) at the core. The idea was that ideas would transmit from office to office, like cells heating up. Fanciful, but maybe true. When the BBC took to employing consultants and the West One project was launched (the TV series *W1A* is close to the truth), some bright spark decided to knock all the interior walls down and paint the vast new warehouse spaces blood red and black, thus rendering them almost impossible to enter without getting a headache or being plunged immediately into depression. So *Start The Week*, *Midweek* and *Stop the Week* (known fondly in-house as 'pluggers', 'nutters' and 'wankers') now shared space with *In Our Time*, *Desert Island Discs*, *Loose Ends* and any number of other weeklies and dailies. The poor sap producing *In Our Time* was therefore audible to the rest of the room when he or she was working on his weekly GCSE notes for Lord Melvyn and trying to find three academics who knew, or were prepared to admit to knowing, slightly different things from the others on the Double Helix, the Salem Witch Trials or Socrates.

The protagonist of my fourth novel, *The Silent Sentry* ('A painfully funny radio psychodrama' the *Guardian*), was a BBC radio producer. The narrative provided rather a jaundiced view of the institution and I was expecting it to become the longest resignation letter in history. My boss managed to get it through the system so it could be published with the proviso that I couldn't be interviewed about it and the book wasn't to make the explicit connection between me and the BBC (thus removing all publicity potential for the book). I forgot the second bit of the agreement and was rightfully told off when the novel came out with a gloomy picture of Broadcasting House on the cover. For much of the latter part of my career I (and the protagonist of *The Silent Sentry*, Maurice Reid) occupied the office behind the clock on the front of Broadcasting House. It was a coveted spot, rather like a potting shed attached to the top of the building. Eight feet square it had a balcony and a pair of French windows which looked out across the Fitzrovia sunsets, while the front window offered a view of the rear of the clock room and a sliver of Regent Street. Because my office had a balcony it tended to be a sanctuary for people wanting a pre- or post-programme cigarette or photographers dragging presenters outside for publicity shots (they still regularly use it for pundits appearing on *Breakfast Time* – it's the one with the church spire visible behind the guest and the grey West End business rooftops). You never knew who was going to turn up and demand access to the balcony but you could set your clock when you saw the *You and Yours* presenter sparking up by the door (11.40 a.m. – *You and Yours* started at midday until it was shifted to 12.15).

Going back to the call from Andreas I allow myself some optimism. For the first time in a long while things on the writing front might be looking up.

24th February

An interesting day in prospect. It seems that one of the editors at the publishers is taking this journal to the editors' meeting today and trying to drum up support for it. I'm not sure how the publishing world operates in this respect, but I imagine it's like the BBC in which a general consensus of enthusiasm has to be agreed before the formal submission at the acquisitions meeting (Weds). Things have moved quickly since I sent this ms off to Tim. He came back from half-term holiday today and seems pleased about developments.

Prompted by continuing reading Raymond Briggs' latest book, I was taken by his delight in using the word 'twerp' to describe somebody, and going on to explain it's a word only an oldish person would use. It led me to revisit Kingsley Amis' definitions from his book *The King's English* of two other terms of abuse, still applicable today: berk and wanker.

Tim chases the publisher for the editor's verdict on the journal at the end of the day but she's out at a conference. *Publishing rule 22: Publishing and politics are the only industries which continue to hold conferences.*

26th February

The journal is being taken to the publisher's acquisitions meeting today. Although I've always wondered what went on at these gatherings I've never been that interested in the process, but this one is important. The prospects for publication of the next novel probably also hang on the verdict for this journal. I google 'acquisition meetings' and find this extract from an editor's blog at Little, Brown:

> 12.15 This is a meeting where commissioning editors present book proposals to the rest of the company – sales, marketing, publicity, rights, finance and legal. They talk through what the book is about and why it would be a good thing for L,B to publish. The other departments give their view and sales say how many copies they would expect to sell in different territories. Then someone from finance will run the numbers and say roughly how much we could afford to pay (as in, what advance we could offer for it).
>
> www.meripaterson.com

Looks like these meetings take place around midday, so the verdict might be delivered by Tim or Andreas today.

2 p.m. No news.

3 p.m. No news.

4 p.m. No news.

At 4.30 I can resist no longer and email Tim. Nothing comes back for a while. And then . . . at 5.33:

All good!!!

Thumbs up.

He's preparing an offer.

Julie tells me she's taking me to the pub to celebrate. They've done up a small Victorian place with low ceilings, wood-panelled walls and candles on the table just round the corner from where we live close to the centre of Brighton. A couple of damp dogs are usually asleep by the bar, there's decent beer, steamed-up windows, clean (ish) glasses. It was sold recently but the company which bought it did it up to look exactly like the old place, but less sticky. It suits us.

9th March

I'm working at the library when the offer for the book comes in to Tim and is then emailed to me. It pops up as I'm serving a woman who is telling me that she comes from the Midlands and her local library has removed most of the chairs to discourage street sleepers from lodging there. When the woman leaves the desk there is nobody left waiting to be served so I open the email. The offer is £7500 for world rights. The previous book went for £10,000 for UK and Commonwealth rights. It's an opening bid. I don't mind. An advance, as noted before, is just that, and if by chance this collection of rambling thoughts somehow finds an audience then it might 'earn out' (i.e., sell enough copies for the advance to be covered so the book then starts earning more money). Probably won't but I'm not sure if the rights include film/TV. I'd welcome a few more producer/head-cold meetings in Soho. It's fifteen years since I last enjoyed one and I miss them. Tim will go back and ask for a bit more. It's part of the dance but he's booked a restaurant for lunch on Thursday with Andreas, which will be great so long as London is not locked down because of the coronavirus. At the moment it dominates the news but we're still in the 'delay' phase.

In the library a customer has complained that the automatic sinks in the washrooms only dispense water for twelve seconds rather than the government-recommended twenty and we should do something about it pronto. The idea of pressing the button twice doesn't seem to be within her capabilities. Trev is alerted to see if the machines have a dial to increase the water allocation.

19th March

The world has changed. Coronavirus has locked down the planet. I'm sitting alone on the ground floor of the vast empty library. The staff are in but the public are not. Occasionally borrowers loom through the rain towards the doors and deposit their books through the massive letter box. They peer into the gloomy interior and then wearily trudge away. There's not much to do here. A few bits of stock processing and a turn on the phones to reassure people that they won't be fined. Some of the calls are from deeply troubled people who just want to offload on the pretext of asking for opening times. The library is no longer available as a place of sanctuary.

In the silence, as I begin to process the ramifications of the offer for this book, I'm taken back to something in the

Quentin Blake exhibition we visited last week. At the exit was a wide cabinet housing four shallow drawers, each of which my grandson opened to reveal a large sheet of card on which was written one of Quentin Blake's reflections. In the bottom one was this:

> There are various . . . stages at which I may have to stop and start again – the drawing may be finished but uncoloured or even completely finished before I decide that it lacks some flavour hinted at in the rough, or that there's some quality of line or colour that doesn't seem quite consistent with the rest of the book. And sometimes I may do two or three finished versions in the search for some phantom felicity. This comes under the heading of Artist's Neurosis, and later I am not always sure why I made the choice I did or if it was the right one.

'Phantom felicity'. It's perfect. Any writer would recognise it: reaching for something complete or perfect that cannot be found, only granted to you.

The journal is done but a writing life is never over, even though the life of a published writer will of course ultimately be. *Like the Living* remains unsold. Perhaps the novel was a necessary stepping stone to this journal. Four first-person narratives. Four versions of myself telling a story about a man looking for a key to unlock his life.

When I worked for the BBC as a radio studio manager, one of the Friday shifts was *Stop the Week*. It involved spending the afternoon and early evening in a large basement studio in Broadcasting House. The first task was to record the topical song, performed by Instant

Sunshine or Fascinating Aida, and then the programme itself, which would be transmitted on Saturday evening. For fifty or fifty-five minutes Robert Robinson would preside over his four eloquent guests who'd riff on some of the more trivial news stories of the week, or be set a task such as trying to come up with six famous people called Stan. The producer was svelte Hungarian émigré Michael Ember. Puffing on his slim panatella, at around fifty minutes into the recording he'd announce to the studio managers, 'I'm looking for an out.' This was the cue for the second SM to wake up and stand beside the tape machine, readying him or herself to play the signature tune, while the panel SM would wait for the signal from Ember, 'Thank you,' to fade the studio voices out under the music. The impression therefore was that although the programme was finished the conversation was continuing.

Like Michael Ember on a late Friday afternoon I'm now looking for an out from this journal. Last night I slept on it and, as many times before, handed the problem over to my unconscious mind. The answer delivered when I woke was to go back to the beginning. So, this morning I opened the tatty file containing my first substantial writing effort – *The Pier Song* – and, for the first time in nearly fifty years, read it:

> Sam awoke. It was almost dawn. He yawned, stretched, and looked forward to the day: Sunday. He looked around him and saw miles of pebbles, broken glass and ice-cream wrappers, dead fish and seagulls and, of course, the pier. The tide was already halfway up the Palace Pier and as Sam glanced up at the clock, his

personal timepiece, he could see the sea roll forward to greet him and then away again accompanied by the anguished screams of the millions of small pebbles dashed against each other under the swell. He stood up and, after he had pulled the rolled-up newspapers out of his raincoat, he picked up his battered guitar case together with a tattered leather bag and sauntered up the worn stone steps onto the promenade, across the wide coast road and into the sleeping heart of Brighton. . .

Not too bad for an academically failing, school-terrified fourteen-year-old. At the desk in my parents' bedroom I had found writing – or it had found me. When I wrote I felt a strange comfort. My fears over my academic failings, the brutality of my teachers, the appalling anxiety I woke with each morning ahead of walking to the school bus, all disappeared. I was on a beach I had never visited with a man I had never met, but knew both so fundamentally that I could relate how it felt, how the man talked and what he dreamed and feared. Unlike in the real world, here was a place I could control and participate in without embarrassment or humiliation. I wasn't afraid in this world – and I've sought sanctuary in it ever since.

There are sixty pages in the folder, but I recognise that it contains the beginning of a story that I have continued to tell for the next fifty years of my life. I know now that however a story masquerades as plot or setting the underlying narrative continues from book to book. And that is where the magic lay – and still lies.

The Pier Song, though, was not just the beginning of my writing journey. It also predicted, perhaps even dictated, where that life would be lived: in Brighton, within a mile of the pier itself. Perhaps I'll finish it one day – or perhaps this journal is the final chapter.

Appendix:
Rejections – a selection

18 October 1979
From the BBC TV Light Entertainment Script Editor

Dear Mr Paling

Thank you for sending me your script *One Week in the Life of Simon Stiles*.

Forgive me, but this isn't within sight of being an acceptable script. On this evidence I can't envisage that you can win over the hundreds of professional authors who devote full time to writing.

It would be hypocritical – and unhelpful – if I said otherwise.

Yours sincerely

———

15 March 1984
From the Editor, Script Unit, Drama Radio

Dear Mr Paling

I am returning your play *Old School Ties* which I regret to say we do not wish to broadcast.

We felt the theme was one that had been explored in various ways rather regularly and that your variation wasn't quite original enough for us to explore it again. In fact we found it a little hard to accept that John would still be so obsessed with Cooper after nearly thirty years; or that a genuine talent would be destroyed by schoolmasterly criticism. Nor were we convinced by Cooper's psychological make-up. The blinding business struck us as a little forced and the revenge on the boy reading to Cooper almost melodramatic. By the way, I would think the play is actually several minutes too long for a 30' slot as it stands.

I'm sorry to disappoint you once more.

Yours sincerely

———

19 March 1985
From the BBC Television Script Unit

Dear Mr Paling

Thank you for allowing us to read your script *Mermaids*. This has now been carefully read and considered but I regret that it has not been recommended for production.

I am returning it herewith.

Yours sincerely

————————

19 September 1985
From the Editor, *Thirty Minute Theatre*, Radio 4

Dear Chris

How prolific you are! We have now read *Call of the Mantelpiece Virgin*.

I think there is a problem with this having started life as a short story. It isn't that there is too much narration but rather that the narration is not really dramatic – it doesn't have a significantly individual tone of voice to put across the character and make us feel we are being spoken to by a personality we are able to get to know. The other reservation about the script is that it somehow doesn't have the gutsy feel that the story and setting seems to demand. The dialogue just isn't rough-edged enough.

I'm sorry for the list of criticisms but I hope they are of some use to you.

Yours

_____

7 January 1986
From the Editor, *Thirty Minute Theatre*, Drama

Dear Chris

I hope Clive passed on to you the information that *Way Station* was very well received by the Department and regarded as a very successful gripping creepy little play.

I'm sorry after the good beginning to have to give you negative news on *Temporary Magic*. I think it was an interesting move to try a completely new dialogue style but because the American idiom is not native to you it does seem a bit off the peg – phrases we have all caught up from American films etc. which are not particularly revealing for your individual characters. Whilst this wouldn't be a problem for some sort of spoof I think it is very unhelpful for this particular play the plot of which is somewhat unlikely and which would only be really convincing if there were a lot of subtlety in the relationships of the characters.

I'm afraid the answer has to be no.

With best wishes,

Yours

———

25 July 1986
From the Editor, *Thirty Minute Theatre,* Radio 4

Dear David Wyatt [I must have used a *nom de plume* after the criticism of being too prolific]

Thank you for letting us see *All Mod Cons* which we have now read and considered. I am sorry to tell you that we are not able to offer you a production of it.

Because of the very great number of scripts under consideration I am afraid it is not possible to give detailed comments on any work but that which we think likely, with revision, to reach broadcastable quality.

Yours sincerely

————————

30 April 1987
From the Editors proposed *Man in Black/Fear on Four* series,
Radio 4

Dear Mr Paling

Many thanks for your suggestion *The Priest House* with regard to the proposed *Fear on Four* series.

We have received a great many entries and the selection towards compiling a hopefully well-balanced series has been no easy task. Judging or anticipating standards of entry have had to be balanced with types of play, period, background, etc., and I am afraid in this particular case both Gerry and myself find that we regretfully have to return your idea to you.

Thank you for your interest and the time taken in helping us.

Yours sincerely

————————

7 July 1987
From the Editor, Fiction Dept, *Woman's Own*

Dear Mr Paling

Thank you for sending us *Heaven* and I apologise for the delay in returning it to you.

I am sorry to have to tell you that due to the fact we are a very small office, we are unable to accept unsolicited manuscripts. I suggest your best course of action is to send your work to a literary agent who is the best person to advise you on the suitability of your work for publication.

I do hope that this has been of help, and I wish you luck with your work.

Yours sincerely

———————

14 January 1988
From the Editor, *Thirty Minute Theatre*, Radio 4

Dear Chris Paling

Thank you for sending *Op. Cit.* which I am returning. I am sorry that we will not be able to offer production on it. Apologies for the delay in returning it, due to the number of scripts received in this office and the change of editorship.

I am afraid our reader did not get on to a wavelength with this. She felt it was competent and professional but that the characterisation and dialogue could have been stronger, and the humour seemed a little forced.

Sorry not to be more encouraging on this one.

Yours sincerely

———

13 September 1988
From the Editor, *Afternoon Play*, Radio 4

Dear Christopher Paling

I am returning the new draft of *Draper's Gazette*. As you now know I have not been able to place the play with a producer. The feeling, as I explained, is that the play is too familiar in its setting, theme and central characters. I do not think a new draft will convince any of us otherwise. I should also say that the second draft looks still too long.

I had hoped that my letter would have reached you before you began work on this. Obviously it got caught up in the mail strikes.

I am sorry I cannot be more encouraging.

Yours sincerely

_____

3 May 1994
From the Publisher, Jonathan Cape

Dear Chris Paling

I am so excited that we shall be publishing *After the Raid*. I thought it was one of the most strange and original novels I've ever read: I can't get it out of my mind.

I proposed to Deborah that she, you and I meet for a celebratory lunch. She thinks it might prove difficult to organise (she's probably right), but do please give me a call and let's at least arrange a day when you and I can meet.

I enclose a copy of our latest catalogue.

With best wishes

'I discovered that rejections are not altogether a bad thing. They teach a writer to rely on his own judgement and to say in his heart of hearts, "To hell with you."'

Saul Bellow

READING ALLOWED
True Stories and Curious Incidents from a
Provincial Library

'Frequently funny, sometimes sad
and occasionally troubling . . . Borrow a
copy from your local library, if you still
have one. Better yet, buy it'
Mail on Sunday

READING

ALLOWED

TRUE STORIES &
CURIOUS INCIDENTS *from*
a PROVINCIAL LIBRARY

CHRIS PALING

'Paling's deftly drawn vignettes are frequently funny, sometimes sad and occasionally troubling . . . Borrow a copy from
your local library, if you still have one. Better yet, buy it'
Mail on Sunday